Arthur Crawshay Alliston Hall

The Virgin mother: Retreat addresses on the life of the Blessed Virgin Mary as told in the Gospels

With an appended essay on the virgin birth of Our Lord Jesus Christ

Arthur Crawshay Alliston Hall

The Virgin mother: Retreat addresses on the life of the Blessed Virgin Mary as told in the Gospels
With an appended essay on the virgin birth of Our Lord Jesus Christ

ISBN/EAN: 9783337259785

Printed in Europe, USA, Canada, Australia, Japan

Cover: Foto ©Lupo / pixelio.de

More available books at **www.hansebooks.com**

THE VIRGIN MOTHER

RETREAT ADDRESSES

ON

THE LIFE OF THE BLESSED VIRGIN MARY

AS TOLD IN THE GOSPELS

With an appended Essay on the Virgin Birth
of our Lord Jesus Christ

BY THE

RT. REV. A. C. A. HALL, D.D.

Bishop of Vermont

.

NEW YORK
LONGMANS, GREEN, AND CO.
AND LONDON
1894

THE CAXTON PRESS

NEW YORK

CONTENTS

ON THE LIFE OF THE BLESSED VIRGIN MARY

PREFACE.

I HAVE been repeatedly urged to publish these Meditations, which in substance have been several times given in Retreats for Women on both sides of the Atlantic. I had thought to write out the Addresses afresh from notes taken on different occasions, but this has proved impossible. The notes which were taken with considerable fulness, but by no means *verbatim*, at a Retreat for the Guild of the Epiphany (a society of Churchwomen engaged in educational work), in the Chapel of the Sisters of Bethany, London, in January, 1892, are here printed, after careful revision as regards their matter, but with manifold imperfection of literary form.

However, the Addresses are intended now, as when delivered, to serve as suggestions for meditation and prayer, rather than as finished discourses. In this way I trust they may prove helpful.

The Essay on the Virgin birth of our Lord Jesus Christ, which is printed as an appendix, was written for a clerical society in the spring of 1891, and was published at that time in *The Church Eclectic*. It gives the grounds for accepting the literal statement of the Creed which is taken for granted in the Meditations.

A. C. A. H.

BURLINGTON, VERMONT,
August, 1894.

INTRODUCTORY MEDITATION.

THE PREDESTINATION OF THE VIRGIN MOTHER.

WE will take for the general subject of our Retreat, as the starting-point of our Meditations, *the life of the Blessed Virgin Mother*, as presented to us in the pages of the Gospels.

So we will think in our several meditations of different scenes and mysteries in her life, as recorded in the Gospels; of her Predestination; her Training for the manifestation of God's high purpose; of the Annunciation by the Angel; of her Visitation; of the Birth of the Holy Child and the accomplishment of the Mystery of the Incarnation; of her Purification and the Presentation of her Child in the Temple; of the Flight into Egypt, and the return to Nazareth; of the scene in the Temple when her Child was twelve years old. Then we will

think of her at the beginning of His Ministry, at the Marriage Feast at Cana of Galilee;
of her standing at the foot of the Cross; of
the absence of her name from those to whom
the Lord showed Himself after His Resurrection; and, lastly, we will take leave of
her in the Upper Chamber, waiting on her
knees in prayer for the gift of the Holy
Ghost.

And in thus directing our thoughts to her,
it will not be so much with the view of considering her unique and personal honour,
but, rather, of regarding her as the type and
pattern of the Church collectively and of
every individual soul in whom Christ is to be
born by the Spirit's power.

So does our blessed Lord place her before
us.   You will remember how it is told us by
St. Luke * that, when He was preaching to
the multitude, a woman, struck by the
power and beauty of His teaching, ex-
claimed with enthusiasm: " Blessed is the
womb that bare Thee, and the paps which
Thou hast sucked!"—and how our Lord

* St. Luke xi. 27, 28.

turned the encomium pronounced on His
Mother:—"Yea, rather," He says, "blessed
are they that hear the Word of God
and keep it." He is not denying His
Mother's honour, but only referring. that
honour and praise to its truest, deepest
cause.

Thus St. Augustine says, "She is more
blessed in that she bore Christ in her heart
by faith, than in that she conceived Him in
her womb according to the flesh." And
St. Ambrose, "According to the flesh, the
Mother of Christ is but one; according to
the Spirit, the fruit which all bear is Christ."
And so you will remember on another occasion, where our Lord is told that His Mother
and His brethren are standing without, de-
siring to speak with Him, He asks, "Who is
My mother, and who are My brethren?"
And, then lifting up His hands over His disciples, He says: "Whosoever shall do the
will of My Father which is in Heaven, the
same is My brother and sister and
mother;"* at once repudiating any merely

* St. Matt. xii. 46–50.

natural relationship that would interfere with His Heavenly Father's work, and at the same time declaring that all may have a share in Mary's highest prerogative.

> Joy to be the Mother of the Lord,
>   And thine the truer bliss,
> In every thought, and deed, and word,
>   To be forever His.

> Ave Maria ! thou whose name
> All but adoring love may claim,
>   Yet may we reach thy shrine;
> For He, thy Son and Saviour, vows
> To crown all lowly, lofty brows
>   With love and joy like thine.

> Bless'd is the womb that bare Him—bless'd
> The bosom where His lips were press'd,
>   But rather bless'd are they
> Who hear His word and keep it well,
> The living homes where Christ shall dwell
>   And never pass away. *

I. It is in this light that we are going to think of the Blessed Virgin— as the pattern and figure of all the faithful; for consider (and we will take this

* *Christian Year.* Poem for the Annunciation.

as the first point in our meditation) how
all the mysteries of Our Lord's Incarnate Life are intended to have their counterpart in the spiritual experience of the faithful. Remember how constantly this thought
is brought before us in the Collects of the
Prayer Book, *e. g.* in those for the Annunciation, Christmas, Easter Eve, and the
Ascension. For us He was born, that we
might be re-born in Him; for us He died,
that we might die with Him to sin and the
world and self; for us He rose, that in Him
we might rise to newness of life; for us He
ascended, that with Him we might also
in heart and mind thither ascend, and with
Him continually dwell. So, pre-eminently,
in the mystery of the Incarnation, Mary's
name stands in the Creed, not merely as one
honoured above all women, but as the pattern
of all in her humility, purity and obedience,
which made her meet to conceive Christ by
the Spirit's power, to become the Mother of
the Lord.

And this very mystery of the Incarnation
is to be re-enacted in our own experience.

How is that? The Son of God, One with
the Father, becoming Man, one of us, of
Mary's substance, by the Spirit's power, is
to be born in *us !* What is our Christian life
for—what are all the Sacraments for, but for
this, that the Glorified Incarnate Son may
take of our substance, our nature, our talents, and may be born in us by grace, that
we may have His Life reproduced in us?
Nothing short of the Life of the Eternal Son
of God—the Holiness, the Purity of God, is
the standard at which we are to aim; *that* is
to be reproduced in our circumstances: the
Divine Perfections are to be translated, reproduced in *our* life, *our* home, *our* trials,
our difficulties, *our* age of the world; He is
to be really and truly Incarnate of our substance! Ah! see how the Incarnation really
gives to us the standard of Christian life.

And this is to be true of every *individual*
experience; not only of the Church, but of
each one of us. Let us ask ourselves, What
is the special likeness of Christ that He
would reproduce in *me ?* What are the features of His Life that He calls *me* to imi-

tate ? What pattern would He set before me in my work, my circumstances, my difficulties ? What are the inspirations of grace that He would urge me to cultivate and cherish ? Ah! I come into Retreat to see how this is to be carried out, how His Life is to be re-enacted more truly than ever in my experience—how He is to be born in me by the Spirit's power.

So we are to think how the Mysteries of Our Lord's Incarnate Life are to have their counterpart in our own spiritual experience.

II. Consider, secondly, *Mary's predestination and ours.*

" Known unto God are all His works from the beginning of the world."* It was probably God's original, eternal purpose that His Son should become Incarnate and assume our human nature, quite apart from the after necessity of restoring that nature, of the beating down of man's foes, and of making reparation for the offence against the Divine Majesty. We may believe that

* Acts xv. 18.

it had ever been the will of the Eternal
Word to become man, to unite the creature
with the Creator, to manifest Himself in the .
flesh. He had manifested Himself in nature
already; He willed a further manifestation
of Himself in man, whom He had made "in
His image and likeness;"* in "the fulness
of time" He meant to be born in man's
nature, and in it to accomplish the Divine
purpose in its fulness, to act out the Divine
Perfections in human circumstances.

And then sin came in and modified that
original plan of Almighty God. It still held
on, but oh, what a change was rendered necessary in the accomplishment of God's Purpose! Think what it would have been, had
there been no sin to meet, to make reparation for. Think how the whole Life of the
Incarnate Son would have been one unbroken
joy; using all His faculties in carrying out
the Father's will; ruling all the world
according to the Father's pleasure! But sin
came in; and it must be conquered, at whatever cost; the ruined nature must be re-

* Gen. i. 26.

paired, Satan's chains wrenched apart; the Seed of the woman must crush the serpent's head, at the expense of His own heel being bruised in the encounter; He must do battle with our spiritual foes and set us free.

But God's purpose lasts on; the same result is attained in the end, though by a different route. Instead of being a Man of Joy from the Cradle to the Ascension, He became "a Man of Sorrows and acquainted with grief," * until the battle had been fought out and redemption won, and He "was crowned with glory and honour." †

Ah! and just so must it be in our own experience. God had a purpose for each one of us, a work for each one to do, a place for each one to fill, an influence for each one to exert, a likeness to His dear Son for each one to manifest, and, then, a place for each one to fill in His holy Temple. And His purpose for us was clear from all eternity; He saw it at the Font of regeneration, when He started us on our course; and then,—

* Isaiah liii. 3.　　† Ps. viii. 5; Heb. ii. 8–10.

alas! alas! how have we to lament the loss
and the misuse of those gifts of nature and
of grace! How have we thwarted God's
purpose, come short of His expectation!

Yet He has not cast us off with our sin;
"He has devised means that His banished
be not expelled from Him."* And, as He
devises means whereby the fallen race may
be brought back to Him through the Passion
of His Incarnate Son; so, in individual lives,
the path of penitence is necessary; we have
to struggle on, in our individual experience,
as did once our great Representative. We
have to come back; God will accomplish His
original purpose, though He will modify
and adapt His plan. His purpose lasts on;
we must rise to that in the end, or who can
say that He will not cast us away? We may
not say, "God's purpose is too high for me;
I cannot rise to it; I will take something
else! That which I might have risen to so
easily, had I been faithful to His inspirations, docile to the indications of His will,
. within and without, is too great for me

* 2 Sam. xiv. 14.

now!" Alas! we have to climb a rough path now, to travel by a more circuitous road; but it will lead to the same goal at last. Praise to His Name! He did not cast us off—

> When all was sin and shame
> A second Adam to the fight
> And to the rescue came!*

It is just the same with our own individual lives. *Penitence*, then, and *Hope*, we may take as the primary lesson of our Retreat. In our self-examination let us see how far, how sadly far, we have failed to correspond with what we knew to be His will for us. Well might we become discouraged and reckless as we look back. But no! Hope comes in to save us from the snare. As a means of reconciliation the Passion of the Incarnate Son came in to accomplish God's purpose and original plan for man. Even so His purpose for me lasts on and shall be accomplished; through penitence and struggle the likeness of the Eternal Son shall be fashioned in me.

* *"Dream of Gerontius."* By J. H. Newman.

III. Once more. Think of God's purpose standing sure and being accomplished, in spite of long delay and many apparent disappointments and reverses. The promise of the Redeemer, "the Seed of the woman," * Who should reverse the defeat which our first parents had sustained at the hands of the enemy, given along with the sentence pronounced on man's disobedience and sin, is clung to by Eve; when Cain was born, she thought, "I have gotten *The Man* from the Lord " †—that seed to which He pointed. Ah ! what disappointment ! In Cain she sees but the aggravation of her own sin; the parents had broken away from love to God, their child from love to his brother. So sin spreads.

So think, as sin becomes worse and worse, how the promise seems further and further off. Yet by the Prophets it is made more and more clear as time goes on. Though so long delayed, in the end the promise of God is found to have stood firm, the "Seed of the woman," the Virgin-born appears;

* Gen. iii. 15.   † Gen. iv. 1.

God has been true to His word. Man needs
to have patience, to be subjected to long discipline; but God never takes back His word.
Remember that text at the beginning of St.
John's Gospel, commonly misunderstood as it
stands in our ordinary version: "The light
shineth in darkness, and the darkness comprehended it not." * We ordinarily understand it of the darkness *not taking in* the light
—not comprehending it—not assimilating it.
Of course darkness cannot assimilate light,
or it would cease to be darkness. The right
meaning is, "the light shineth in the darkness, and the darkness *overcame it not*"—as
we read in the margin of the Revised Version, "*did not overtake it.*" The idea is of
a little flame shining in the darkness, and
the gloom around seeming now and again to
threaten to extinguish it. But it is not overwhelmed, it shines on; and at last the light
blazes forth and illuminates the world. Yes;
the Word of God is "the light which lighteth
every man that cometh into the world." †
He shines, however dimly, in every man's

* St. John i. 5. † St. John i. 9.

reason and conscience, amid all their darkness, prejudice, disobedience and sin, while
it seems continually as if the darkness were
about to extinguish that little flickering
spark of light. So was it with God's promise. At the time of the Flood all flesh had
" corrupted his way upon the earth,"* and
yet God's word holds on; the light revives.
Israel goes into Egypt; and it seems as if
the promise given to Abraham is to be overwhelmed in Egyptian darkness and sin. But
no; it lasts on; the light appears to die out,
but it is seen again. Again in the Babylon-
ish Captivity all seems to be swallowed up;
but no, it lasts on, it is not overwhelmed;
when the world was at its darkest and drear-
iest, things right themselves; and then, at
last, the light blazes forth to disperse the
darkness, though Israel is given up to the
hope of an *earthly* Messiah, and only just a
few, like Simeon and Anna, Mary and
Joseph, and the disciples of the Baptist, are
waiting for redemption in Israel, the promise
is fulfilled, the Seed of the woman comes at

* Gen. vi. 12.

the expense of His toil aïd Passion to work
out man's redemption.

And so is it in our individual experience.
That illuminating light of conscience, quick-
ened by regenerating grace, seems in some
of us, at times, to be all but blotted out. But
no; that inspiration which pursued us so lovingly, in spite of all our disregard of its
warnings, shining out now and again, through
the sins of our life, is not extinguished; it is
still there, it would not let us have peace; it
is capable of being fanned into a burning
flame which will disperse all the darkness
around. Think, then, as you prepare for a
review of past experiences, of this wonderful,
long-suffering patience of God, bearing with
us individually, as with the human race
collectively; learn from it patience in dealing with others, hopefulness with regard to
those who are committed to your charge;
and when all seems to be going wrong,
when all seems to be dead, hold on to them
still, as God has held on to you. The little
spark—O cherish it; there is something good
in that child; hold on to it; that spark is not

overwhelmed yet; nay, with careful cherishing it shall yet burst out into a flame, and,
in God's good time, disperse the surround-
ing gloom.

Learn, then, the lesson of patience and
hopefulness, from Mary's predestination and
ours, from God's purpose, and, in the end,
its sure accomplishment. "Wait for the
vision;" and "though it tarry," still, "wait
for it;" for, in the end, "it will surely
come."*

One more lesson in connection with, and
in illustration of, the same truth. Have
you ever noticed in this light the genealogy
at the very beginning of St. Matthew's Gospel? Sometimes one has wondered at the
long list of names, dry and uninteresting,
standing at the forefront of the New Testament—what business has it there? Ah!
just look. It does, indeed, stand in the forefront of the Gospel, full of " good news " for
those who have eyes to see! Run through
these names; choose out the female names;
there are four before you come to the name

* Habak. ii. 3.

of Blessed Mary, and each one has a horrid blot. There is the name of incestuous Tamar; of Rahab, the harlot; of Ruth, one of an accursed nation; and of Bathsheba, the adulteress, who had been the wife of Uriah. Through that stained genealogy, the Holy Seed comes! God shows us that He can bring out of a stained line a perfect work; that He *can* "bring a clean thing out of an unclean;"* the light is not swallowed up in darkness; the promised Seed of the Woman has come—the Incarnate Word of God.

We look back upon our past life, like that stained record, that blotted genealogy, on sins of one kind and another—of wasted opportunities, of carelessness and of indifference, and we are tempted to despair; we think, "What is the use of my trying, of my cherishing a high standard? I had better give up!" No; at the end of that stained record, that blotted genealogy, stands the name of the Virgin Mother of the Incarnate Son, of Him who came to

* Job xiv. 4.

save His people from our sins, to change the
course of our life, to purge away our earthly
stain, to make us pure instead of earthly,
disciplined instead of self-indulgent, gentle
and meek instead of wilful and wayward.
Think of the promise of God standing sure;
think of the perfect holiness, at last revealed, the work of the Spirit to sanctify
all our sin-stained descent—a gift that
has washed away that which soiled our
life.

Yes; there are sure mercies awaiting us,
if only we will return. Think of the words
of the Prophet Jeremiah: " Thus saith the
Lord . . . . Ye shall seek Me and find
Me, when ye shall search for Me with all
your heart."*

Let me give the Scripture references for
the passages I have quoted:

i. Our Lord's words concerning His Blessed Mother, as
the type and pattern of the faithful.—*St. Matt.* xii. 49, 50;
St. Luke xi. 27, 28.

ii. And in connection with those words of Our Lord, the
words of St. Paul about the reproduction of the Birth of
Christ in our own experience.—*Gal.* iv. 9; *Ephes.* iii. 17.

* Jer. xxix. 10–14.

iii. The verse about the Light 'shining in darkness, and the darkness overwhelming it not.—*St. John* i. 5.

iv. The stained genealogy.—*St. Matt.* i.

v. God's promise of His sure mercies to those who desire to seek and to return, and to those who seek Him with all their heart.—*Jer.* xxix. 10–14.

And now, with the thought of God's purpose concerning Blessed Mary, and of His purpose for ourselves; of His purpose known to Him from the beginning; of His knowledge of us, both in His predestinating love, as He would make us, and as we really are, let us kneel and repeat Psalm cxxxix.

SECOND MEDITATION.

LET us meditate upon the training of Blessed Mary. Contemplate her as a child, studying the Old Testament Scriptures.

Almighty God, Who hast a work for each of us to do, a place for each of us to fill; have mercy upon us, we beseech Thee, as we draw near to Thee, lamenting all our unfaithfulness and our want of correspondence with Thy holy will. Help us to yield ourselves in loving trustfulness to Thy holy leading; grant us to know what Thou wouldst have us do; and give us grace and power faithfully to fulfil the same, that so we may grow in Thy knowledge and love; through Jesus Christ our Lord. Amen.

Our Father.

We take for our leading thought through-

out our meditations the example of Blessed
Mary as the type and pattern of all the faith-
ful in whom Christ is to be formed by the
Spirit's power.

In our Introductory Meditation we thought
of Blessed Mary's predestination, and of
ours; of God's eternal purpose, and how it
was accomplished; and of His will for the
manifestation of His Son in us. Now we
will go on to consider *her training for her
vocation, and ours.*

In thinking of her childhood and early
years, there is room, of course, for a wide
range of imagination; legend has been busy
concerning her youth. We will leave all
that on one side. All through the Retreat
we will try and keep close to the Gospel
record. Three points, however, are dis-
tinctly suggested by the thoughtful consideration of St. Luke's narrative of the
Annunciation and Visitation—three points
which throw light on Mary's previous history:

1st. Her preparation. "The Lord *is*
with thee." *

* St. Luke i. 28.

2d. Her previous dedication of herself to God's undivided service, implied in her response to the Angelic Salutation.

3d. Her knowledge of God's Word, shown in the *Magnificat*.

I. First, we will consider *Mary's unconscious preparation for her vocation*, which yet God knew all along.

From the first He had had His purpose; "the seed of the woman should bruise the serpent's head." *

He foresaw her, He foreordained her, He was watching over her, He was preparing her; but, all the while, she grew up in perfect unconsciousness of the great vocation which was in store for her. If it could be said of St. Paul that he was "a chosen vessel;"† of Jeremiah, "Before I formed thee in the belly I knew thee; and before thou camest forth out of the womb I sanctified thee, and I ordained thee a prophet unto the nations;"‡ and of John the Baptist, that he was sanctified from his mother's womb;§ so

* Gen. iii. 15.   † Acts ix. 15.
‡ Jer. i. 5.   § St. Luke i. 15.

surely we may apply to Blessed Mary those
words, "from the bowels of my mother hath
He made mention of my name."*   Accordingly, not only her Nativity, but her Conception also is commemorated by the Church,
although the manner of her sanctification is
not defined.   God did not choose her because she was naturally fitted, but He fitted
her because He chose her.   He always fits
and prepares those whom He chooses, if only
they will be true and faithful to His purpose
as He makes His will known to them, step
by step.   *Deus coronat dona sua in nobis.*
It is God's own gift that He crowns in us,
not only in heaven, but on earth, as each
grace is given in reward for some previous
grace corresponded with; and that previous
grace is the gift of God.   So Mary was
"*filled with grace;*" not "full of grace" as
a *source*, but filled with grace, as a *choice
receptacle.*   God Himself had been preparing her; she herself, all the while, perfectly
unconscious; growing up in Nazareth, living
her simple child's life "as a lily among

* Is. xlix. 1.

thorns," * growing up sweet and beautiful in
that rough place of evil repute, concerning
which it was said, "Can any good thing
come out of Nazareth?" †—that little pro-
vincial town, notorious for the lawlessness
and depravity of its inhabitants; "unknown" to earth, "yet well known" to
heaven; God watching over her, preparing
her; and Mary all the while unconscious.

So is it with each one of us. God has
His purpose for each one. We do not come
into the world at haphazard to find some
place to fill, some work to do; God has His
plan for each one; "known unto God are
all His works from the beginning." ‡ He
has arranged our circumstances, our environment, our inheritance, our combination of
talents, the presence of this gift, or the
absence of that—all have been taken into
account by God, ordered and overruled by
that Wisdom which "reacheth from one
end to another, mightily and sweetly order-
ing all things." §

* Cant. ii. 2.   † St. John i. 46.
‡ Acts xv. 18.   § Wisdom viii. 1.

Going back to our earliest years, think
when we were Baptized, incorporated into
the Body of Christ, how He gave us our
name and place in His regenerate family.
Our Baptismal name is sacramental; not
only because it tells of our regenerate position, but it is itself a sort of sacrament, an
outward sign of a great spiritual reality; it
tells of the special purpose God has for each
one of us, of the likeness to His Well-be-
loved Son that He would have produced in
us, as Christ is born in each of us by the
grace of the Holy Spirit. And, by degrees,
as life advances and develops, that name,
which expressed God's purpose for each, is
spelt out, syllable by syllable, almost letter
by letter, till we come to know fully what
that name stands for. At our Confirmation
or our First Communion; at some great
upheaval of our life, some disappointment,
sorrow or trial; or when spiritual things
first shine out as very real, *e.g.* at our first
Retreat or our first Confession, God shows
us something of what He would make of our
life—of what we should do with the powers

He has given us; we learned a fresh syllable,
as it were, of our Baptismal name. We
learn that there is something we can do—
some place we are to fill—yes, and something, perhaps, that is shut out from us;
that we are *not* intended for this or that.
"I am learning God's purpose and mind for
me." And so, in deeper spiritual things—
by the advice of friends, the warnings and
counsels of spiritual guides, by the voice of
conscience—in all these ways God is making
more plain what He would have me seek after,
what special features of His Son's Life He
would have me reproduce. It is only gradually revealed; in mercy He withholds all
that He sees we could not yet bear. It
would startle us and stun us were we to
know all that is before us; the height of our
vocation would overwhelm us; were we to
see the difficult steps by which that height is
to be attained, it would cause us to despair!

Did we but see
When life first open'd, how our journey lay
Between its earliest and its closing day;

Or view ourselves, as we one time shall be,
Who strive for the high prize; such sight would break
The youthful spirit, though bold for Jesu's sake.

But thou, dear Lord!
Whilst I traced out bright scenes which were to come,
Isaac's pure blessings, and a verdant home,
    Didst spare me, and withhold Thy fearful word,
Wiling me year by year, till I am found
A pilgrim pale, with Paul's sad girdle bound.*

So it was with Blessed Mary. Had she known the unique honor for which she was intended, the prerogative that should be hers, that she should be the Mother according to the Flesh of the Eternal and Only Begotten Son, she must have shrunk back dismayed. But she was gradually led on:—"What I do, thou knowest not now, but thou shalt know hereafter."† Ah! how many meanings those words of our Lord have! The way by which God leads us seems often to be so dark, so puzzling, so unmeaning! Those trials, those perplexities—why are they? "Thou shalt know hereafter" what this or that was meant for—this check, that disappointment—"what I do"—the urging on to

* J. H. Newman, in *Lyra Apostolica.*   † St. John xiii. 7.

this or that way of perfection which would
have raised you from earthly hopes to something higher; or the warning voice, which
if you had followed you might have avoided
this or that habit which did not destroy, perhaps, but which marred and lowered your
spiritual life, blurred the conscience, and
kept you back from perfect truthfulness,
perfect purity!   Alas! "thou knowest not
now, but thou shalt know hereafter"—not
only in another world, but here, as we wake
up and see how, if only we had been faithful
to God's voice, we might have been saved
this or that stain, this or that wound, which
can only now be healed by long and severe
discipline of penitence.   Ah! if I had only
followed this or that inspiration of conscience—been true to those means of grace—
made the most of those educational advantages—how much more capable I might
have been now; how much more I might
have effected, not only for myself, but for
others!   I see now what I might have become but for my own disobedience or negli-
gence or disregard of warnings.

"What I do, thou knowest not now."
Yes; and there is a brighter side to this.
As we look back and see this or that thing—
this little disappointment—that little trial—
how God wove it into our life, how it fitted
in with God's great purpose, and by it we
were led on to something better and higher.
Think of Blessed Mary being led on, step by
step, and all unconsciously. "The Lord *is*
with thee," the Angel said, and therefore He
can come to thee in closer and more wondrous fashion.

What is needed? Just one thing on our
part—fidelity, loving correspondence. He
knows what He is working for, and it shall
surely be accomplished, if only we do not
thwart His purpose. "Whosoever hath, to
him shall be given."* Step by step we are
led on, by a real process of evolution, one
grace giving birth to another, each step
making the next more easy and more natural; each step we *miss* making the next
more difficult. Ah! let us look back and see
God's dealings with us, praise Him for His

* St. Matt. xiii. 12.

loving care and providence, bewail our want of correspondence with His leadings, and brace ourselves with loving earnestness for whatever we have now to do, however hard and difficult, to make up for our past failures.

II. *Think of Mary's previous dedication of herself to the service of God.* It seems clear from her response to the Angel, "How shall this be, seeing I know not a man?"* that she had as a girl dedicated her maidenhood entirely to God's service; otherwise her response has no meaning. If she had been just about to enter upon the marriage state under its ordinary conditions, the promise of a child would have been natural. She might have wondered how it could come about that she should have the honour of being the mother of the Messiah; but she asks, "How shall this be," that I become a mother, "seeing I know not a man?"

It is not an inquiry of scepticism or doubt, like that of Zacharias, but of true and modest testing of the Angelic message.

* St. Luke i. 34.

The promise fires all her ambition, but how
can it be harmonized with her previous vow
—the entire dedication of herself? In
prayer and meditation she had learned of a
closer spiritual fellowship with God, and
for this she had risen above the great ambition of Jewish women, to be, at least, in the
line of the Messiah's maternal ancestry. It
was this hope which made a single life or
barrenness to be considered a curse or a
disgrace among Jewish women. Mary had
risen above that; she had foregone that
great hope; she looked for "a place and a
name better than of sons and of daughters;"*
she had consecrated herself wholly to God
that she might wait upon Him without dis-
traction. And *because* she had foregone
that great hope, *because* she had responded
to a higher call, and sought a deeper spiritual grace, God gives her the other blessing
also; she shall be the Virgin Mother of the
Messiah, of God's Incarnate Son!

And so in our own life we must be separated from lower things; not only from

* Is. lvi. 5.

things that are wrong and bad, but from things that are in themselves innocent and good, but which might prevent our rising up to things greater and higher.   Blessed Mary is separated from the world before she is consecrated to God; and so must it be with us. This applies not only to the dedicated life of "Religious."   In many things, in one way or another, we may, any of us, have to give up some great hope, some possibility, some sphere of influence that opens out before us; we might have it, we might keep it, but, somehow, we feel it would not be quite consistent with our dedication to God.   "I am kept back from this or that opportunity— this or that cherished plan of advancement in the world—this or that development of my faculties and talents by a higher duty to which God has called me.   I have to work for those near and dear to me.   I might get on in this or that sphere of usefulness, but I am held back by conscience; I must give up something good for something that is really better."

God, be sure, is never outdone in generos-

ity.   " There is no man that hath left house,
or brethren, or sisters, or father, or mother,
or wife, or children, or lands, for My sake,
and the Gospel's, but he shall receive an
hundredfold now in this time, houses, and
brethren, and sisters, and mothers, and children, and lands, with persecutions; and in
the world to come eternal life." *

Think of the sacrifices to which God has
called you in the past; see how they have
been blessed; how God has led you on by this
or that dedication of yourself or of your talents, to something higher and better.

Bishop Jeremy Taylor, in his " Golden
Grove," advises us to make note of four
great extraordinaries in our lives, and in our
seasons of special spiritual exercises to bring
them out before us.

i. The great and shameful sins into which
we may have fallen, in order to excite a
deeper repentance for them.

ii. The greater and more excellent acts of
virtue that, by God's grace, we have been
enabled to perform, in order that we may

* St. Mark x. 29, 30.

learn what we *can* do now, by God's grace, from the consideration of what we have done in the past.

iii. The more singular graces and blessings He has vouchsafed to us, to kindle our loving gratitude.

iv. The special vows and promises we have made to God; that we may consider how far we have been true and faithful, in the past, and set ourselves to greater faithfulness in the time to come.

Dwell on that second point. Consider what God has enabled you to do in the past. Don't in coming into Retreat dwell too much on the shame and humiliation our sins have brought upon us; there must, of course, be the humbling of ourselves as we come face to face with the past; but hope—look up; your past may be a pledge of what God will do for you in the future. Think of the grace He has given you, the holy inspirations He has breathed into you, and how "He who has begun a good work in you will perform it," if only you are true and faithful.*

* Phil. i. 6.

III. Consider *what must have been Mary's study of God's Word in her early years*, as shown by the *Magnificat.* At the Visitation, when St. Elizabeth saluted her with such reverence, "Blessed art thou among women, and blessed is the fruit of thy womb. And whence is this to me, that the mother of my Lord should come to me?"* Mary at once breaks out into her song of thanksgiving—the evening Canticle of the Church throughout all ages—the *Magnificat.*

And the *Magnificat* is all based upon Hannah's song of thanksgiving, as recorded in 1 Sam. ii. Mary does not try to be original, her mind is steeped in Holy Scripture; the spiritually-minded Hannah inspires Mary, and the more spiritually-minded Mary knows how to make the words her own, to adapt them and apply them with fuller meaning and in thanksgiving for a greater Gift than that which called forth Hannah's song of praise. All that comes from Mary's lips wells up from her heart, but all is based on

* St. Luke i. 42, 43.

the Old Testament psalm. The Spirit uses His former utterances; the *Magnificat* is the New Testament edition of the Old Testament canticle.

Consider how our mind and heart ought to be familiarized with God's former utterances; how in joining in the Divine Liturgy, the Psalter, and in all the utterances of the Church, we ought to be learning, not merely phrases of devotion for our own devotions and private use, but how they should be to us a real means of approach to God, and we should adapt them to our own personal use. "He that hath an ear, let him hear what the Spirit saith to the Churches."* Let the Spirit bring our minds into harmony with the minds and hearts of the saints of all ages. In this text we have the reconciliation of two truths that nowadays are so often thought to be contrary—the Spirit speaking to the Church generally, and to ourselves individually. What the Spirit saith unto us will be in harmony with what He has said to others; we can test what we think He says

* Rev. ii. 29.

to us by its harmony with that which He has said to others.

And this applies to the use of manuals and books of devotion; let us seek to be absolutely real and natural in our use of them. It matters not how good they are, whether Bishop Andrewes', or Bishop Cosin's, Bishop Ken's, or Bishop Taylor's—their words are not our own, and in many instances perhaps are too high for us, we have not yet risen to them. Use them if you please, but do not be content with just using them; adapt them, assimilate them, appropriate them. A manual of devotion that is used just as it is printed is not worth much; it ought to have ever so many lines scratched out, and many others written in; it must be adapted and assimilated by different persons according to their several needs. Ah! make your prayers real! "I am approaching the Living God. He has His intention, His mind, His vocation for *me*. I am to approach Him in my devotions with *my own* needs, and sins, and joys, and hopes."

So take these three points for meditation,

drawn from the story of the Annunciation and the Visitation:

i. *God's preparation of Blessed Mary for her vocation;* her previous training, her gradual preparation for it; herself, meanwhile, all unconscious; God working out everything to its great end.

ii. *Her previous dedication of herself.*

iii. *Her study and application of God's word;* giving us an example of reality in devotion, in drawing near to God.

Let us repeat Psalm xxv.

THIRD MEDITATION.

THE ANNUNCIATION OF THE BLESSED VIRGIN MARY.

LET us meditate on the Annunciation.

Behold the Angel coming with his lofty salutation to Mary in the lowly home of Nazareth:—" Hail, thou that art highly favoured, the Lord is with thee: blessed art thou among women." And Mary, as she surrenders herself to the Divine vocation, says, " Behold the handmaid of the Lord; be it unto me according to thy word." *

O Almighty God, Who hast fashioned us to carry out Thy purpose, that Thy Son might be manifested in each one of us; grant us each one, now and ever, to listen to Thy voice and so to yield ourselves to the operation of Thy Blessed Spirit that we may indeed be conformed to the Image of Thy Blessed Son, that Thou mayest be glorified

* St. Luke i. 28–38.

in us, and that we may find acceptance with Thee at the last, through the same Thy Son Jesus Christ our Lord, Who liveth and reigneth with Thee and the Holy Ghost, ever One God, world without end.   Amen.

We have meditated on the training and preparation of Blessed Mary for her great vocation.   We come now to consider the story of the great crisis of her life, when (1) the Angel announced God's will and purpose for her, and (2) Mary responded, "Behold the handmaid of the Lord; be it unto me according to thy word."   And then (3) the consequence followed, the Divine purpose is accomplished—"the Word was made flesh," of her substance, "and dwelt among us." *

Let us consider in the story the three great lessons of: i. Her prudence; ii. Her consent; iii. Her self-oblation.

I. *Consider the Prudence of Blessed Mary.*

Think of her first recorded word.   Truly, she realized the description in the Book of Proverbs of the virtuous woman who

* St. John i. 14.

"openeth her mouth with wisdom, and in
her tongue is the law of kindness"*
"She openeth her mouth with wisdom."
The Angel comes with his lofty salutation, "Hail, thou that art highly favoured,
the Lord is with thee: blessed art thou
among women;" and Mary, in her modes-
ty and lowliness, is troubled at his salutation, "and cast in her mind what manner
of salutation this should be." She is ut-
terly unconscious of the high dignity, the
wondrous destiny that awaits her. The
Angel goes on with the promise of a Son;
"Fear not, Mary, for thou hast found
favour with God. And behold, thou shalt
conceive in thy womb, and bring forth a
Son, and shalt call his name Jesus." And
then she is perplexed and she asks, "How
shall this be, seeing I know not a man?"
The question is not one of scepticism or of
doubt; but of modest inquiry, of a desire to
test before she accepts the Angelic message; and so it is treated in an entirely different way from the question of Zacharias,

* Prov. xxxi. 26.

"What shall be the sign?" In condescension to his weakness God gives him a sign; but the sign manifests God's displeasure at his unbelief; he is struck dumb; he goes out of the temple unable to speak, or even to bless the people in God's Name; he can only make a sign. When at the child's circumcision he acts in faith and obedience, and gives the name which the Angel had foretold, he recovers his speech.

There is nothing of this in Blessed Mary; she only wonders how this great and blessed promise can be reconciled with her existing obligations. Her espousal to Joseph is only for the shelter and protection of her dedicated maidenhood, and she cannot understand the wondrous promise until the Angel explains that it shall be accomplished with no violation of her holy estate:—"the Holy Ghost shall come upon thee, and the power of the Highest shall overshadow thee,"* etc. Then, as soon as the way is made clear, and the difficulty removed; or, rather, when the promise is seen not to conflict with

* St. Luke i. 35.

her obligations, immediately follows her entire self-surrender; without hesitation she replies, "Behold the handmaid of the Lord; be it unto me according to thy word." *

Now we are to imitate Blessed Mary in her *prudence*. When suggestions come to us, whether of doctrine or of practice, we are to *test* them. When some new form of service, some new rule of devotion or of self-discipline, or some new belief is presented to us, we are not to swallow it down with one tremendous gulp,—nothing of the kind; we are to ask the question, How is this to be? How is this new belief to be reconciled with what God has already taught me? Can this idea be reconciled with the obligations that are already laid upon me? We are to be on our guard lest we be seduced (as was Mother Eve) by Satan transforming himself into an angel of light and coming to us with messages flattering to our self-love. Do not swallow down as true everything you hear in a sermon; test it. The Bereans were commanded when they searched the Scriptures

* St. Luke i. 38.

to see "whether these things were so." *
And St. John says we are to " try the spirits
whether they are of God." † So with this
message—Is it from heaven—an angel of
God—or is it a seducing spirit ? Is this fair
promise to lead me aside from the strict path
of duty or obedience ? Our reason must
always justify our obedience. This is not
rationalistic; reason is never contrary to
faith. What is faith, after all ? It is but
reason illumined by the Spirit of God.
Faith reveals to us that which reason alone
could never guess; or faith makes certain
what reason made very probable. Faith and
reason can never contradict one another;
reason and conscience are God's voice in the
human soul, and God can never contradict
Himself. The Word, who is Incarnate in the
fulness of grace and truth, is "the Light
which lighteth every man that cometh into
the world." ‡ Faith is like a telescope, which
enables us to see distant objects which the
naked eye could never discern, or which it
could only see dimly and in outline. So

* Acts xvii. 11.   † 1 St. John iv. 1.   ‡ St. John i. 9.

faith enables to see clearly that which reason only has a glimmer of. Faith never *contradicts* reason, nor creates the object which it reveals any more than the telescope *creates* the object made visible in the distance.

Just so is it with regard to matters of practice. We may be so easily deceived. This or that spiritual project comes before us— some suggestion of greater strictness, perhaps; and yet it may be only to foster pride. We overreach ourselves, undertaking something that we can never accomplish; or we undertake some distant duty, neglecting that which God has placed close to us in our family or with our friends. " From the *deceits* of the world and the flesh and the devil, good Lord, deliver us! " From self-love, and from all that leads us aside from the plain path of duty and obedience, good Lord, deliver us!

Our Blessed Lord's Temptation shows us the need of this testing, for to such temptations He was exposed; for instance, to anticipate the close of His Fast:* to claim protec-

* St. Matt. iv. 3, 6, 9.

tion in a way not promised; to snatch at power for a good use, but not in God's way.

How often are we deceived like Mother Eve, instead of putting the question, like Blessed Mary; so that, when that is answered, we can go on to the second step. "Now, I know this comes from God, so I must go on and do the will of God." What we take up lightly we let go lightly; but if we pause and test the matter, then we shall have ground and cause for obedience.

But how may we test these things and be delivered from self-deception?

We have two safeguards. 1. By cherishing a spirit of constant faithfulness. "My sheep," says our Lord, "hear My voice."* They *are* My sheep already. When I come to the sheepfold and call, they recognize My voice. And why? Because they have so often heard it before. Yes; as we listen and obey, we learn to distinguish the voice of God from all other voices; from that of our own self-love, and from all seducing spirits.

* St. John x. 27.

It is as when we hear.the voice of some dearly-loved friend in the midst of a crowd, it sounds above all other voices, it rings out distinct and clear—"I know that voice; I have heard it so often before; I could not mistake it." Just so it is with the faithful soul; it has gained, by listening and obeying, the power of discerning God's voice from all other voices; it has learned to distinguish it from the seductive voices of the world. So constant faithfulness gives us the power of recognition and discrimination.

2. Again, what God says will always be in harmony with what He has already said; for God cannot contradict Himself. The new vocation, the new teaching, which comes from Him, will be the legitimate development (not the contradiction) of previous teaching; it will be consistent with all that has gone before. He will not call in different ways. True, He may keep us waiting, and by so doing He may be preparing us for His call to enter upon something in the future that we cannot yet take in hand, and we have to wait until the outward tokens of His

Providence correspond with the inward call of Grace; then, when the two coincide, we have a perfect moral assurance. For instance: A young woman thinks she has been drawn by God to devote herself to the Religious Life; yet at present she has other duties to fulfil. In her home, perhaps, there are younger children to teach and care for; or parents who need her aid and sympathy; or perhaps the express will of others hold her back; she has checks. Then she has no right to enter upon this new experience. Let her by all means cherish the thought and keep herself free from other ties; she may be training herself in exercises of prayer and self-discipline for a more entire dedication of herself; but not, remember, by acting as a sort of demi-semi Sister of Mercy with rules and practices unsuited to her actual position, instead of being a loving sister or a good daughter in the world. Do your duty perfectly, soundly, in whatever state God has placed you, and then you will be ready to be called on to whatever else He has in store for you.

And so with the call to the Priesthood. There is an earnest desire in a young man to devote himself to the ministry; but he has not the intellectual gifts, or the training necessary for it; and so he is held back. But the thought has not come to him for nothing, and it is not to be lightly put aside; no, it is intended to lead him on to some higher self-dedication, to a more recollected, devoted life, to whatever God may have in store for him. We may be mistaken as to the outward form in which any call is to be realized, but its inner spiritual significance remains.

So think of those two safeguards with which we are to be armed against deluding self-love, and enabled to discern God's will for us, as we consider the example of Mary's *prudence*, as she asks, " How shall this be ?" *i. e.* how is it to be reconciled with existing obligations ?

II. Let us go on to consider her answer in her second word, and learn a lesson from her *Consent*.

Having been assured, she says "Behold the handmaid of the Lord; be it unto me according to thy word." *   It was in Mary's power to have refused.   The Incarnation might have been delayed, and another instrument would have to be found, furnished and prepared for God's work.   The Creator will not act in this great mystery without the creature's full consent.   The Omnipotent stands on ceremony with his own finite creature; He waits for Mary's consent.

Yes; God has raised us to too great a dignity to use us as mere blind instruments for His purpose, whether for the carrying out of some great *external* work, or for the accomplishment of His work *within* the soul.   He has bestowed on us the awful but blessed prerogative of Free Will.   Here is the explanation of that which so often perplexes us about temptation.   "*Why* does God allow evil?   If he wants me to be good, *why* does He allow it to be possible to be bad?"   The answer is plain: We cannot be really good without the possibility of

* St. Luke i. 38.

being bad. We might serve God with all the mechanical obedience of the heavenly bodies; but the simple obedience of a little child is immeasurably above that, because it is not a mechanical but a *moral* obedience. So God would have us become good by *choosing* goodness, not as slaves, but as friends, who *choose* justice, goodness, obedience, and so become just, good, and obedient. *We become that which we choose.* So did the blessed Angels become good; they passed through their probation, they chose God, and they stood firm in grace; the others refused—refused God as the Law of their being, and they are forever parted from Him.

And so man has to choose, throughout the probation of his earthly life. God never forces our will. He comes to us, as He sent the Angel Gabriel to Blessed Mary, waiting for our consent; as He came to Matthew at the receipt of custom; he was called to follow Jesus, he might have remained a tax-gatherer, but by an act of willing obedience "he left all, rose up and followed Him."* So

* St. Luke v. 28.

was the rich young man called; the choice was given him, he was unwilling, and so he was allowed to go away sorrowful.* So was Judas called. The Master spent on him all His loving care; he falls away because he was not "obedient unto the heavenly vision" granted him.† God never, never forces our will. Herein is *holiness*—in doing the will of God, in being conformed thereto; herein is *sin*—in withholding self from the will of God. It matters not what the subject-matter may be; it may be in some tremendous struggle, or in some trifling concern that the choice comes; if conscience tells us this or that is wrong, and we do not heed, it is the breaking away from the will of God. The vocation comes, God speaks plainly, lovingly, entreatingly, but He won't constrain us; He will have the homage of our loving choice.

Think of this as true, not only in the great crises of life, in times of some moral upheaval, some great conversion, but it is likewise true in the continual actions of daily life. It is true, also, as regards our recep-

* St. Luke xviii. 23.   † Acts xxvi. 19.

tion of sacramental grace. The Angel
comes, as he came to Blessed Mary, that we,
like Blessed Mary, may yield ourselves in
order' that God's work of grace may be accomplished in us; but we must work along
with God. We thought of the necessity of
real, personal communion with God in
Prayer; so must it be in the reception of
the Sacraments; they do not act as charms;
they have their place, they are means to
ends, but they are not ends in themselves.
Never confound means with ends. The
Sacraments are the covenanted means of
grace, but we must " open our mouth wide "
if we would be filled; we must come with
right dispositions, we must " hunger and
thirst after righteousness," * if we are to be
filled. Thus, for instance, in making confession; it is not the mere going, or the
recounting our sins that avails; we must
come with real sorrow and desire for pardon; we must for our part put away the sin
by true repentance that Almighty God may
put it away on His part by an act of forgive-

* St. Matt. v. 6.

ness and cleansing. Absolution will never stand in place of contrition. There is no more deadly snare than confession without repentance. There is an old Latin motto which says: *Tanta gratia quanta dispositio*— the grace we receive will be in proportion to the dispositions with which we come. "Open thy mouth wide, and I will fill it." * We must yield ourselves to the operations of the Holy Spirit; laying the skin of our soul bare, so to speak, that the Finger of God may touch and heal and cleanse it.

So think of the lesson of Mary's Consent —her yielding of herself to the Divine vocation.

III. *Think of the Self-Oblation of Blessed Mary, and what that consent involved.*

She must have foreseen something of what the acceptance of the Angel's message involved. In her study of the prophetic Scriptures she must have gained some real knowledge of what the Messiah was to be, and of the nature of His work. She had not a

* Ps. lxxxi. 10.

mere earthly conception of His career, such
as the Scribes and Pharisees had. She must
have known that the Messiah was to be "a
Man of Sorrows and acquainted with grief."*
She must have known that the shadow of
the Cross would fall on those near to Him,
that the Mother of the Man of Sorrows must
be the *Mater Dolorosa;* that, in some way or
another, the sword would pierce her own
soul.† She must have seen, too, in rapid
forethought, what the acceptance of the
Angel's message involved for her in the near
future—the shame—the hard thoughts—the
suspicion of her fall—ah! how exquisitely
painful to her pure soul! But it is God's
call, and at whatever cost it must be
obeyed. Yes; think what was involved in
those words of self-surrender. "Be it unto
me according to thy word." Mary accepted the sacrifice of that which is dearer to
a young maiden than her very life, and here-
by she becomes pre-eminently the heroine of
Isreal, the ideal daughter of Zion, the perfect type of human receptivity in regard to

*Is. liii. 3.   † St. Luke ii. 35.

the Divine work. She shows herself to be indeed a true daughter of Abraham, the father of the faithful, ready to go forth wherever God directs, even to unknown lands—to darkness, perplexity and shame ! *

So we, too, have to yield ourselves to the Divine vocation; to a greater strictness of life, to some work of charity, some fuller manifestation of the truth of God, at the expense of obloquy, at the cost of separation from those near and dear to us—and God knows what it costs us to cut ourselves off from them! Yet it must be done; we must act, like Blessed Mary, on the principle of faith, leaving consequences to Him. Mary could not see how she was to be carried through or provided for; but she knew that He was faithful who had called her, and she placed herself in His hands. Is there any more comfortable word in Holy Scripture than this:—"Faithful is He that calleth you, who also will do it." † Because He is faithful, strength will be given sufficient to carry out that which is commanded.

* Godet on St. Luke's.   † I Thess. v. 24.

There must be neither eager, vain, presumptuous snatching at high things; nor a cowardly holding back when God calls.

We will test the suggestion that comes to us. When once we are assured that it is from God, there is only one response we can make,

"Behold the handmaid of the Lord, be it unto me according to thy word!"—"Lord, what wilt thou have me to do?" *

With such thoughts let us repeat Psalm xvi.

* Acts ix. 6.

FOURTH MEDITATION.

THE VISITATION OF THE BLESSED VIRGIN MARY.

LET us meditate upon *the Visitation of the Blessed Virgin Mary*. Contemplate Mary singing the *Magnificat* in the house of Zacharias and Elizabeth.

O Almighty God, Who hast called us near to Thyself in the covenant of grace, and hast bestowed upon us countless gifts of grace, grant us, we pray Thee, so to meditate on all Thy goodness that we may return to Thee the homage of our loving gratitude; and, praising Thee for Thy mercy in the past, may learn to trust Thee for the time to come.

Our Father.

All the subjects on which we have already meditated in connection with the early life of the Blessed Virgin Mary—her predestina-

tion, her training, and the Annunciation—
all these belong to the *Joyful* Mysteries of
the Incarnation, as they are called, as dis-
tinguished from the *Sorrowful* Mysteries, in
which she shared the Passion of her Son; as,
in the *Glorious* Mysteries, she shared His
Triumph.

And the mystery of the Visitation, on
which we are now to meditate, is pre-eminently a Mystery of Joy. Mary hastens to
communicate her wondrous joy to her cousin
Elizabeth, and to congratulate her relative on
the joy that has come to her after such long
waiting. And Elizabeth welcomes St. Mary
with reverent joy. "Blessed art thou
among women, and blessed is the fruit of
thy womb. And whence is this to me that
the mother of my Lord should come to
me?"* Her unborn child recognizes the
unborn Saviour, and at Mary's salutation
the babe leaped in his mother's womb for
joy; while Mary bursts out into her canticle
of joy—"My soul doth magnify the Lord
and my spirit hath rejoiced in God my

* St. Luke i. 48.

Saviour." The whole visit is a time of joy, beginning and ending with a canticle; beginning with Mary's *Magnificat*, and ending with Zacharias' *Benedictus*, in which he poured out the result of all those meditations which had filled his mind during that nine months solitude and silence, in which he had been, as it were, keeping his Retreat, pondering the ancient prophecies which the Angel told him were about to be fulfilled; and in the fulfilment of which his promised son was to play so prominent a part as the herald of the Messiah. Dwell upon the holy joy of those three months which Mary spent in the house of Zacharias and Elizabeth; think of the converse between those holy souls during that time.

So let us think of Mary's joy, and of its lessons for ourselves.

I. *Consider the Magnificat as the expression of her joy*, called forth by Elizabeth's recognition, which gives a sanction, as it were, to what the Angel had said, and by which Mary's own faith is confirmed.

And Mary's joy is to be a lesson of joy for us:—

> Our Lady sings Magnificat
> In tones surpassing sweet;
> And all the Virgins bear their part,
> Sitting about her feet—

not merely in heaven, but in the kingdom of heaven on earth. Mary is the cantrix of the Church on earth, and all saints take up the canticle which she begins—"My soul doth magnify the Lord." The *Magnificat* is the first canticle of the New Testament, standing in the Gospel story before Zacharias' *Benedictus*, or Simeon's *Nunc Dimittis*, or the Angels' *Gloria in Excelsis*, just as it begins each festival in Church, as "the evening and the morning are the first day,"* giving tone and key, as it were, to all the days of our life.

Think of Mary singing the *Magnificat*, (1) as the representative of humanity, the second Eve; (2) as the representative of the Church, in thanksgiving for the Incarnation. Think of her singing the *Magnificat* as an

* Gen. i. 5.

act of praise for all the gifts of grace and for the hope of glory vouchsafed to us. (3) Think of her singing the *Magnificat* as an act of homage, of *personal* thanksgiving for the great things God had done for *her*.

And with her we are to join in singing *Magnificat*, (1) for all humanity; (2) for the Church collectively; and (3) for ourselves individually.   Two great causes for personal joy are shadowed forth in the *Magnificat*, for Mary and for us.

i. It is the expression of Mary's *joy for what God had done for her in His choice of her;* for her unique privilege of being the Mother of the Incarnate Son—"all generations shall call me blessed."

And so for ourselves also.   Think of our vocation, of God's predestination and election of us, to be born in a Christian land, within reach of the Sacraments and means of grace, to a growing and fuller appreciation of all the treasures and fruits of grace stored up in the Catholic Church.   Think of our sheltered homes, our educational advantages, our spiritual privileges. And what am I, that I should have been singled out to be born in a Christian land rather than in Central Africa, and in the Catholic Church rather than under some imperfect system; that I should have been baptized in infancy and brought within reach of all the gifts of grace provided for me? "Ye have not chosen Me, but I have chosen you." * What am I, that such loving kindness should have been shown to *me?* Do we thank God for the gifts of grace which surround us so commonly, or do we take them as a matter of course? Do we join in the thanksgiving, that God has "called us to the knowledge of this grace and faith in Him?" †

> Jesu, what didst Thou find in me,
> That Thou hast dealt so lovingly?

ii. Then think of the second great cause of personal joy, for ourselves as well as for Blessed Mary.

It was her act of praise for the beginning

* St. John xv. 16.　　† Baptismal Service.

of God's work in her, and she is confident that He will accomplish and perfect that which He has begun.

And we are to thank Him for what He has done in and for us; not only for His gifts of grace all around and about us, but for His work *within*. As we thought in an earlier meditation, and as Bishop Jeremy Taylor tells us, we are not only to meditate on the shameful sins into which we have fallen, but we are also to praise Him for all the acts of virtue we have been enabled by His grace to perform. Ah! yes; don't think it humility to disparage grace, but thank God for what He has done in and by you; don't shut your eyes to it; it is the part of true humility to look every fact in the face, to see it in its true light; to recognize every gift of nature and of grace, and then to realize our responsibility for the right use of all, our responsibility to God from whom they come, and to our fellow-creatures for whom they are bestowed. It is not humility to shut our eyes to any, fact. Yes; " He that is mighty hath done to me great things"—

Mary refers all to Him—"and" therefore "holy is *His* Name."

St. Paul recognizes this, how God had worked in Him; he had "laboured more abundantly than all" the other apostles—"yet not I, but the grace of God which was with me." *

Learn, then, the lesson of *thanksgiving*. It is due to God, it is due to yourselves. Thanksgiving for the past makes us trustful in the present and hopeful for the future. What He has done is the pledge of what He will do. You notice how St. Paul, in all his epistles, after his introductory salutation, thanks God for all that He has already done in those to whom he had ministered; and then, in the strength of that thanksgiving, he is full of assurance that He who has begun a good work in them "will perform it until the day of Jesus Christ." †

See how in the Lord's Prayer, before we ask anything for ourselves, we are taught to say, "Hallowed be Thy Name." We are first to thank God for what He has done;

* 1 Cor. xv. 10.   † Phil. i. 6.

and then, after this, we go on to ask, in simple, childlike trust, for all we need.

Our petitions are often so faint because our thanksgiving is so lacking. What strength should praise and thanksgiving bring into our lives! What causes for thanksgiving we have! shelter and protection in our early years, opportunities and advantages for preserving our innocence and cleansing us from evil! Both are due to "God our Saviour," in whom we rejoice. He recalled me when I wandered. He received me when I returned; He raised me when I fell, He upheld me when I stood. "My soul doth magnify the Lord."

Think, then, how our life ought, indeed, to be a life of joy, brought so near to God. "The joy of the Lord is your strength." *

Think of those words from Nehemiah as affording a sort of antiphon to the *Magnificat*—the Song of Christian life—"the joy of the Lord is your strength." Ah! cherish that thought. Don't let your Christian life

* Nehem. viii. 10.

be sad; don't let it create an impression of sadness or gloom on any around you.

Think of the Offices and Services of the Christian Church, how full of joy they are. Think of the great Eucharistic Feast, wherein we show forth in glad exultation Christ's Death and the great things He hath done, and thank Him for His Glorious Resurrection. And in the Offices of the Church, what a large proportion of praise there is in the Psalms and Canticles! And then, in the strength of that praise, we offer supplications. The law of worship is to be the law of life. We are to go forth from the worship of the sanctuary to render the service of our daily life; Mary's *Magnificat* giving the key to the Christian life as it stands in the very forefront of the New Testament—to a life of *joy*. The Christian life should be "steadfast in faith, *joyful through hope*, and rooted in charity." *

That is the mark impressed on it from the very first, at the Baptismal Font. How often have we been untrue to it! Even in

* Baptismal Service.

our penitence there is to be joy; however far off we may have wandered, even to a far country, yet when we have set our faces to return, and are turned in the right direction, the gleams of light from our Father's Home will shine through the darkness of the night; and, looking toward the Father's Home, we may be glad even in our penitence. "I will arise and go to my Father." *

II. *Consider Mary's joy overflowing at the Visitation.* She hastens on the hint of the Angel to Elizabeth, as the old Collect for the festival of the Visitation says, "for mutual consolation;" she congratulates her cousin on the joy that has come to her; and gives her cause for still higher joy, as she tells the Angel's message to herself.

In the *Magnificat* Mary's joy soon passes from the thought of herself, to that which all generations are to gain through her, to what God will do for His people through her and by her. And here we are to learn a lesson:

* St. Luke xv. 18.

as the joy of the Lord enters into our lives we are not to be selfish, to hug our own joy. "Ah, I can thank God—I am safe!" The experiences vouchsafed to us are not to be for ourselves only, but for others. Think of St. Paul's words, "Whether we be afflicted, it is for your consolation . . . . . or whether we be comforted, it is for your consolation and salvation."* Yes, *all* our experiences are to quicken our sympathy for others—that we may be able to impart to others that which God has bestowed on us. Think of what St. John says: "These things write we unto you . . . that your joy might be full."†

That is the very law of the Church's mission, for every man and woman in the Church —to do our part to call others into the same fellowship in which we are seeking to abide, to lead others to the means of grace we ourselves prize, to warn them against the dangers the reality of which we have ourselves learned, to lead them along paths we ourselves are treading.

* 2 Cor. i. 6.   † 1 St. John i. 4.

Think of the years of education, the talents, the influence, the sheltered home, the
protection in early years that have been
vouchsafed to you in order that you may impart your knowledge and influence, your
purity and faith to others also. All our gifts
of nature and of grace are bestowed upon us
for our mutual good. This is true Christian
Socialism; not the silly Communism that
would drag all down to one mean level; but
the recognition that all gifts coming from a
common Father, are bestowed for the common good of all the children of that Father.
All our gifts are to be exercised and culti-
vated for the good of all; we have no business to use and keep any for our own selfish
gratification, but we are to use all for the
common good. Others have a right to expect from us what our common Father has
bestowed on us. They have a right to share
my joy. We are stewards of God's manifold
gifts, which are all bestowed for the common good. So let me ask myself, "Have I
done this? Has my Christian joy, my faith,
my education, overflowed like Mary's joy to

others ?" See how the spirit of the Incarnate Saviour was at once shown forth in Mary. He came down from Heaven to earth "for us men and for our salvation," that we "might have life and have it more abundantly."* He fills her with His own Spirit of love. "In her tongue is the law of kindness." And we, too, are to be Christophers—Christ-bearers—bringing Him to gladden others' lives. Think of this in guild-work, in parish-work, in any missionary enterprise. I, like Mary, am to carry Christ to others, that, as the spirit of the Incarnation was shown forth in Mary at the Visitation, so the power of the Incarnation may be shown forth in my contact with others, as in hers, as we bring Christ to them, and Christ brings life and joy.

"When Elizabeth heard the salutation of Mary, the babe leaped in her womb for joy."† Yes; there is to be no selfishness, no isolation in our Christian life, we are to rejoice in others' good. So think of the mutual consolation of Blessed Mary and

* St. John x. 10.　　† St. Luke i. 44.

Elizabeth. "Come hither and hearken unto me, all ye that fear God, and I will tell you what he hath done for my soul."* That is the spirit of the Visitation. Christ in me is to overcome my natural shyness. We English people have a healthy dislike to cant, we don't wear our hearts on our sleeves; but we stand in the opposite danger of having a false shame in matters of religion. Let us try to put aside our natural reserve and shyness, and be ready to communicate to others that which we value for ourselves, that which makes life tolerable amid all our sorrows, that which has given us light in its dark places, that which has cheered us when otherwise we should have sunk down in sorrow and despair. "O praise the Lord with me, and let us magnify His Name together."† This is the spirit of the Visitation.

III. *Think of Mary's joy in the midst of outward sorrow* as exemplified by her *Magnificat*.

* Ps. lxvi. 16.   † Ps. xxxiv. 3.

Ah! it is all well enough in that quiet, contented home in Hebron, with sympathizing friends to whom an Angel has been with a message of joy. But soon she is to go back to Nazareth, to face the shame and disgrace that awaited her—Joseph's suspicion, the finger of scorn pointed at her by that rough, rude population—" ah ! she is no better than others !" Yet she sings *Magnificat;* she trusts herself to God's loving care, because " tribulation worketh patience, and patience experience;"—what we *have* endured teaches us what we can endure; and experience begets hope, and that hope will not fail or disappoint us because of the "love of God shed abroad in our hearts by the Holy Ghost which is given unto us." *

Think of cherishing that spirit of "joy in the Lord" in the midst of outward sorrow; in temptation, in failure, in times of anxiety or bereavement, of dulness of faith; still protesting the most real belief in spite of deadness of feeling; showing that true love is deep down in the will, not merely on the

* Rom. v. 3-5.

surface of the emotions. While "without are fightings, and within are fears,"* the *Magnificat* is still the utterance of the Christian heart, just as every day—on Ash Wednesday and on Good Friday just as much as at Christmas and at Easter—the Church sings *Magnificat* at Evensong, in different tones indeed and with different antiphons and settings, but the *Magnificat* is never to be put out of our life; in our joys and in our sorrows we are still to look up and "magnify the Lord, and to rejoice in God our Saviour." To look around may cause dismay, to look up brings rest and peace.

And *when* is the *Magnificat* sung? Why, as evening is drawing on, and the shadows close in, and earthly joy and brightness fade away: that is the time to sing the *Magnificat*, and let "joy in the Lord" be the strength of our lives; "hidden secretly in His tabernacle from the strife of tongues;" † like Paul and Silas at midnight singing praises to the Lord, ‡ and their

* 2 Cor. vii. 5.   † Ps. xxxi. 20.   ‡ Acts xvi. 25.

praises opened the prison doors. Ah! how often that may be true in our lives. The prison-house seems fast, and difficulties are insurmountable; but only let us sing and praise God, and the doors are open and a way is made for us to escape. "At midnight," said the Psalmist, "I will rise and give thanks unto Thee." * "Rejoice in the Lord alway, and again I say, Rejoice!" †

i. Think, then, of Mary's joy, and of the *Magnificat* as giving the key to the Christian life.

ii. Of her joy overflowing to others, giving us the pattern of communicating and sharing our gifts with others.

iii. Of Mary singing the *Magnificat* in the midst of anxieties, teaching us, in whatever circumstances we find ourselves, to look up and "rejoice in the Lord."

Let us say Psalm ciii.

* Ps. cxix. 62.   † Phil. iv. 4.

FIFTH MEDITATION.

THE BIRTH OF OUR LORD JESUS CHRIST OF HIS VIRGIN MOTHER.[*]

LET us meditate upon *the Birth of Our Lord Jesus Christ of His Virgin Mother.*

Behold the stable-cave of Bethlehem, where Mary, when the days were accomplished, brings forth her First-born Son, and wraps Him in swaddling clothes, and lays Him in a manger. And listen to the song of the angels as they throng around in wondering adoration, "Glory to God in the highest, and on earth peace, good-will towards men." [†]

By the Mystery of Thy Holy Incarnation, by Thy Holy Nativity, good Lord Jesus, deliver us from our earthliness, from the lust of the flesh, from the lust of the eye, and from the pride of life. Conform us more and more to Thine own Likeness, as

[*] See Essay in the Appendix. [†] St. Luke ii. 6–14.

Thou dost make us, by Thy gifts of grace, partakers of Thy Divine Nature; that in Thee we may find acceptance with the Father, both now and at the last; with Whom, in the Unity of the Holy Ghost, Thou livest and reignest One God, world without end. Amen.

Our Father.

In the old Service Books the Office for Christmas Day contained a " Memorial of St. Mary at the full accomplishment of the Mystery of the Incarnation." And these are the words of the Antiphon:—" Behold, all things are fulfilled which were spoken by the Angel concerning the Virgin Mary."

"The days were accomplished that she should be delivered." *

Nine months have passed since the Angel came with his wondrous message; the Eternal Word has been enshrined within her; the Holy Ghost has gradually fashioned of her substance that Human Body with all its faculties and powers, and the Word has

* St. Luke ii. 6.

been " made Flesh."* The Creator has assumed a created Nature. It is a mystery before which we can only bow in adoration; and yet this mystery is the pattern of our own spiritual life; the historical mystery of the Incarnation is to have its counterpart in our own spiritual experience. And so we will meditate on the Birth of Our Lord Jesus Christ of his Virgin Mother, and its spiritual lessons; we will consider the truth of the Incarnation and how it is to be re-enacted in us.

We will see how to build up ourselves, our moral and spiritual life, upon the foundation of our most holy faith.† We shall note the value of clear, dogmatic expression of the truth, as we carefully consider certain points of doctrine and the lessons contained in them.

What is the truth of the Incarnation?

There are four great points we have to keep in mind, and each has its spiritual lesson for our life.

i. He who is born is Very God, of One Essence with the Father.

---

* St. John i. 14.   † St. Jude xx.

ii. He is Very Man, of the substance of the Virgin Mary, His Mother.

iii. These two Natures, the Divine and the Human, are indissolubly linked together in the Unity of His One Divine Person.

iv. All this is accomplished by the operation of the Holy Ghost. The Only-Begotten Son of God is " conceived by the Holy Ghost, born of the Virgin Mary."

Let us consider each of these truths, for its practical importance.

I. *He who is born is Very God, of One Essence and Being with His Father.*

Mary is truly the God-bearer—Theotokos. This title was contended for by the Church, not so much for *her* honour, as to protect the truth of the Incarnation. She is the Mother, according to His Human Nature, of Him who is God. Yes ; it is not the highest of created intelligences that is born of her; then the gulf between creature and Creator had not been bridged over; then Heaven and earth had not been really united. No; it is God who shows Himself in our nature; the Very and Eternal Son of God, "by whom all things were made." He, and none other, "was made Flesh and dwelt among us," and manifested a glory that could belong to none other than "the Only Begotten of the Father, full of grace and truth."* He gives us by the Incarnation a twofold revelation; He shows us what God is, and what man, made in God's Image, should be. "The glory of God," says St. Paul, "shines forth in the face of Jesus Christ."† We know now what God is because we know what Jesus was; and what Jesus was on earth, that God must ever be, in His hatred for sin and His love for the sinner; He has translated into language that we can understand, the language of human conduct, the Divine perfections. We know now what the Love of God is—it means self-sacrifice and compassion; the Holiness of God—it means readiness to suffer anything rather than swerve from true obedience. "See in My Life," Jesus Christ says, "See in My Death, the witness, the testimony to the Divine Na-

* St. John i. 14. † 2 Cor. iv. 6.

ture!" Yes, from Jesus, and from Jesus
alone, we can learn with absolute certainty
what God is; and we learn what man, made
in God's Image, may be. Man was made in
God's Image that he might be conformed to
God's Likeness.

Just consider for a moment—it is a painful thought, and yet it is well to face it—
consider the absolute impossibility of God
assuming the nature of any created being
lower than man. He could not have become
incarnate in any irrational being, for there
would have been nothing for God to fill up;
there would be no correspondence between
the creature and the Creator. God, who is
Love, can only take the nature of one who,
as a moral being, is made in His Image and
is capable of reproducing that Love. Man
can do this because of his natural capacity for corresponding with the Divine
Nature.

Let us learn from this a true missionary
zeal: to do all that we can both at home and
in the world, by prayer and by labour, to
win men to their restoration to God's Image,

to be conformed to His Likeness. " O God of all the nations of the earth, remember the multitudes of the heathen who, though created in Thine Image, are perishing in their ignorance; and grant that by the labours and prayers of Thy Holy Church, they may be delivered from all superstition and unbelief, and brought to worship Thee through Him whom Thou hast sent to be our Salvation, the Resurrection and the Life of all the faithful, Thy Son Jesus Christ our Lord." *

And what does this mean for ourselves? We are made partakers of the Divine Nature. We are not partakers of a holy *man*, but, as St. Peter says, " *of the Divine Nature;* " † we are made, really and truly, "children of God." This is no mere expression of fondness, but it tells of actual relationship. Not that we are made partakers of His Infinity, or of His Eternity, but of His Moral Nature—His Justice, His Love, His Purity, His Righteousness. These I am to set before me; nothing short

* St. Francis Xavier. † 2 St. Peter i. 4.

of this; this is the standard for Christian life. So in my daily life I am to ask, " How would *Christ* have acted in my circumstances ? How would He have me act ? How would *Christ* fulfil my duties, do my work, fill my place, meet my difficulties, turn to account all my capacities and opportunities ?" This is to be the law and inspiration of my whole life; not only of my outward acts, but of all my inward thoughts and desires. There is to be a manifestation of the Divine Nature in *me*.

II. *The Eternal Son of God, of One Nature with the Father, was made Very Man, of the substance of the Virgin Mary His Mother.* " He took not on Him the nature of Angels, but He took on Him the seed of Abraham." * He was really and truly made Perfect Man, of His Mother's substance, having a likeness to her; really and truly deriving from her that Body in which He lived, in which He died, in which He now reigns; the Holy Spirit fashioning

* Heb. ii. 16.

that Sacred Humanity of His Mother's substance. Not only was He Son of Man, but
"of the seed of Abraham," and "of the seed
of David." * He had a real strain of ancestry running down to Him.

(1.) Consider how He was made " Perfect
Man." Taking, first, all the different elements of our human nature; not merely a
Human Body, but a reasonable Soul; a Mind
with memory, understanding, and imagination; a Heart with every true human affection, of love, and of hatred against evil. He
loved His Mother, His friends at Bethany;
He loved His own specially chosen friend, St.
John, His bosom companion, with a particular, individualizing love.† He looked around
with anger and indignation at the hardness
of heart and hypocrisy of the Pharisees.‡
Affections of joy and sorrow belonged to
that Human Heart; He rejoiced with exceeding joy, and His Soul was "exceeding
sorrowful, even unto death."§ " For the

---

* Rom. i. 3.   † St. John xi. 5; xiii. 23.
‡ St. Mark iii. 5.
§ St Luke x. 21 ; St. Matt. xxvi. 38.

joy that was set before Him He endured the Cross, despising the shame."* "Who in the days of His flesh, offering up prayers and supplications with strong crying and tears unto Him that was able to save Him from death, was heard for His reverence."† Every true human affection was found in the Sacred Heart of Jesus Christ, Very God and Very Man.

And every affection of ours is to be sanctified, not one cut off; every one is to be baptised, christened, exercised in true Christian energy.

And He had a Human Will, so distinct from the Divine Will, with which, nevertheless, it ever beat in harmony, that He could say, "Father, not My will, but Thine be done."‡

So every element of our nature, every faculty of ours, from the lowest to the highest, is to be brought under the control of religion; no one part of it is to be left outside; the body is to be trained for God's service, the mind disciplined and brought under the

* Heb. xii. 2.   † Heb. v. 7.   ‡ St. Luke xxii. 42.

yoke of Christ, the affections chastened, the will is to be at once strengthened and controlled. All the different parts of our life—home-life, social-life, our work and our prayer—all the subject-matter of life is to be penetrated with religion. Is this so, in all the details of my life? Or am I leaving religion for Sunday, and letting domestic matters remain outside its influence? Am I careless in my accounts, unpunctual in my duties, untidy in little matters? With a Christian we might almost say the difference between "secular" and "religious" is abolished. "The Word," than which naught is higher, "is made flesh," than which naught is lower, so that "whether we eat or drink, or whatsoever we do" we can "do all to the glory of God," because we can do all in the Name and after the example of Jesus Christ, the Incarnate Son of God.*

Think, then, of this law of sanctification for the whole of human nature and the whole of human life.

* 1 Cor. x. 31; Col. iii. 17.

(2.) Again; the Son of God was made Very Man, Perfect Man; not only assuming our nature in its integrity, but taking it and using it according to the laws of human nature, and so, subject to its *limitations*. The finite is not made infinite because the Infinite Person used it. There were restrictions in His Life as Man. In His human nature He could die; He needed food and rest; He was subject to fatigue. Why should people find a difficulty in accepting any limitations to our Lord's Human knowledge? He, the Eternal Word, knew all things; but why should we shrink from the thought that, as the Almighty *Power* of the Eternal Word was restrained so that it did not at all times overflow His Body, and miracles were not the ordinary law of His Life, but were reserved for great moral occasions; so it was with the Infinite *Wisdom* of the Eternal Word; it was restrained from overflowing the Human Mind? For the purposes of His mission His Mind was Divinely illuminated. Christ came to teach the truths it concerned man to know; about

God—His Being and Character; about man—
his origin and destiny, the true standard of
his life, his relation to God and means of
approaching Him; all this it was necessary
for us to know. But Christ did not come to
teach all those subjects that are on the bor-
der-land, so to speak, of religion—historical,
scientific matters, and so on. His mission
was to teach *religion*, and for that purpose
He inspired His Human Soul.

So think how, in our individual life, we
are to accept the limitations that Almighty
God has imposed upon each of us. It is an
accepted fact that all cannot do the same
thing; all have not the same powers, mental
or bodily. We are responsible for using the
gifts that He has given us. Christ is to be
manifested in *our* nature, in *our* gifts, in *our*
limited sphere and capacities, whatever these
may be. There is one limitation we must
all accept. We are not presumptuously to
overtax our strength, or to disregard our
health, or the dangers which may come from
overstraining mind or body, heart or spirit.

Again. He became Very Man, Perfect

Man, passsing through all the stages of human life and development. He was subject to the law of growth; His body grew in stature, His mind likewise advanced in wisdom—St. Luke says so, and more—that He not only "increased in wisdom and stature," but also "in favour with God and man."* There was a moral and a spiritual development in the Humanity of the Eternal Son. Does this startle anyone?   Is it inconsistent with His being Very God? Why? Everyone will at once acknowledge the difference between the perfection of innocence—the blamelessness of childhood—and the perfection of ripened manhood when temptation has been met and overcome.   There is a peculiar and attractive sweetness and grace attaching to the innocence of a little child; and yet, if that life be cut off in childhood, we feel that something is lost; that innocence might have developed into mature development; there has been no budding forth of all those gifts and graces that existed in germ.

Just so was it with Jesus Christ.   His Hu-

* St. Luke ii. 52.

manity was flawless from the first; from the cradle it was perfect according to God's original design; all was in perfect correspondence with the Divine Will, every impulse of that nature was holy; yet Holy Scripture tells us that "He learned obedience by the things which He suffered."* He was perfected through suffering; He manifested an experimental perfection; He met temptation and overcame it, and so developed the contrary virtues. That Human Nature was more and more made the Instrument of the Divine Will, in obedience to which He increasingly manifested fresh graces and virtues, as "through the Eternal Spirit He offered Himself without spot to God." †

Just so is it to be with our life; we must be content to grow to perfection; we must be humble and we must be patient; we can't become saints all at once; we can't fly from earth to heaven; no, we have to climb rung after rung of the ladder, passing from stage to stage; we must be content to

* Heb. v. 8.   † Heb. ix. 14.

be first "babes in Christ," fed with milk and then with solid meat.* How often we ignore this law with ourselves and with others! How impatient we are with those committed to our care in matters of secular learning! or in matters spiritual, in dogmatic teaching; perhaps we ourselves have just grasped some point, and now we cannot think how others can be so stupid, so blind, as not to see what is clear to us! We are not content that others should *grow*. We need patience with ourselves and with others; we are apt to want to be great saints, or nothing at all!

Ah! Jesus gives us the lesson:—"First the blade, then the ear; after that the full corn in the ear." †

See how this is represented to us in the Sacraments. Baptism is styled by our Lord, "the New Birth,"‡ *i.e.* it is the planting of the germ of spiritual life, which is to be carefully guarded, watchfully cherished, and by degrees developed.

---

* 1 Cor. iii. 2; Heb. v. 13, 14.　† St. Mark iv. 28.
‡ St. John iii. 3.

Again, the Sacrament of Christ's Body and
Blood is our spiritual food. Food is to be
assimilated, and by it we gradually gain
strength. We sometimes hear it said that
"one Communion is enough to make a
saint!" Well, if one Communion is enough,
one Communion was not intended to make a
saint. If God had so intended, the Blessed
Sacrament would not have been given us as
"food," and under the outward form of the
ordinary daily food of the people of the land
—bread and wine. It is the "Bread of
Life,"* Jesus says; and by receiving Communion after Communion our spiritual life
is to be nourished, strengthened and developed; our sinful bodies being made clean by
contact with, by being interpenetrated by,
His own Sinless Body; and our sin-stained
souls more and more washed in His most
Precious Blood; He, more and more, by His
grace dwelling in us; and we, more and
more, by faith, by obedience, by love, dwelling in Him.

So the lesson we learn from this thought

* St. John vi. 33.

is *Patience*—patience with ourselves and with others; and *Humility*. This we may well learn from the consideration of our Lord in His Sacred Humanity gradually growing up to perfection.

III. Let us consider, shortly, *how the Two Natures, the Human and the Divine, are joined together in One Person.* "Not by confusion of Substance, but by Unity of Person," as the Athanasian Creed says.

Yes, so is it, remember, in the Blessed Sacrament. Note the analogy between the Incarnation and the Holy Eucharist. It is a common devotional expression to speak of "the *miracle* of the Blessed Sacrament. It is, really and truly, no miracle at all. It is a *mystery*. A *miracle* involves the suspension of the ordinary laws of nature by the intervention of some higher law. But this is not the case with the Blessed Sacrament. If the Bread and Wine, according to the common, vulgar idea of Transubstantiation, ceased to be, were changed into the Body and Blood of Christ, if one natural substance took the place of another natural substance, this would be a miracle; as at Cana, when the water was made wine; or, supposing our Lord in the wilderness had done as Satan suggested, and changed the stones into bread; this would have been a miracle. There is nothing of this in the Holy Eucharist. The Bread and Wine remain exactly what they were before; their taste, touch and smell are the same, and they are liable to decay. For purposes of nature, for the nourishment of our lower life, they remain precisely what they were before. But by consecration by the Word and Spirit of God they are made vehicles for enshrining and communicating another and a higher Substance, *i.e.* the Body and Blood of Christ, to be the nourishment of our spiritual life. "The bread that we break, is it not the communion of the Body of Christ? The cup which we bless, is it not the communion of the Blood of Christ?"* It is the consecration and taking up of earthly elements to serve a heavenly and spiritual purpose.

* 1 Cor. x. 16.

And just so is it in the Incarnation.
There is no *miracle*, but a great *mystery* in
the Union of the Divine and Human Natures
in One Person. God is not changed into
man, and the Manhood is not made Divine;
but Human Nature, in its perfection, is
taken up into the Divine in the Person of
Christ, without any change or impairing of
His original dignity. And He acted in that
Human Nature in strict conformity with its
laws. The only *miracle* about the Incarnation was in the Virgin Birth—in the manner of His entrance into the world.*

And just so it is in our own spiritual life.
" I am crucified with Christ; nevertheless I
live, yet not I, but Christ liveth in me."
The communication of grace does not take
the place of my personality, it does not extinguish my human life; but it is given to me
to enable me to live more truly—a true human
life; to live indeed under restraint, the " old
man is crucified; " but I am not destroyed by
that crucifixion of my old nature; "never-

* See *Bible Teachings* (on St. John vi.) by the Rev. R. M.
Benson, ch. xxiii.

theless, I live " more truly, more fully, more freely, "yet not I" according to my own natural impulses and desires, "but Christ liveth in me," the real motive and power of my life, " and the life which I now live in the flesh I live by faith in the Son of God, who loved me and gave Himself for me." *

IV. One point more. *The Union af the Divine and Human Natures in the Person of the Eternal Word is effected by the Spirit's Power.* Christ was "conceived by the Holy Ghost, born of the Virgin Mary." Mary was His sole earthly parent; and so the entail of original sin is cut off.

Here we have the one difference between our Lord's Human Nature and our own. In Him there was simply the development of holiness, the going "from strength to strength," from one virtue to another; there were no rebellious elements to restrain, no wrongful tendencies to overcome. In *us* "the flesh lusteth against the spirit, and the spirit against the flesh."† With us

* Gal. ii. 20; Rom. vi. 6.   † Gal. v. 17.

there must be not only the formation of good habits, but the undoing of evil ones; the "putting off" more and more, of "the old man," the "putting on," more and more, of "the new."* So we have this additional reason for cultivating humility and patience.

Ah! life is so difficult, so hard, because we have to bear the consequences of past sins. It is so hard to keep from wandering thoughts in prayer, because I have let my imagination have its own way. I have allowed this or that evil thought, contrary to love, or to purity, or to humility, to get possession of my heart, and now it claims its place there; it has to be put out by force. I have to unravel the tangle of my past life, as well as to weave habits of holiness.

"Conceived by the Holy Ghost, born of the Virgin Mary." Yes; it is not by human or by natural means that the birth of the Son of God in our nature is effected, either in the historical Incarnation, or in its spiritual re-enactment in our own experience. "As many as received Him, to them gave He

* Col. iii. 9, 10.

power to become the sons of God, who are born, not of blood, nor of the will of the flesh, nor of the will of man, but of God." * There is the counterpart in our spiritual experience of the miraculous conception of Him who was "born of the Virgin Mary." " Not by might, nor by power, but by My Spirit," saith the Lord of Hosts."† The Angel came with the message, and Joseph had to guard both the Mother and the Child; but neither Gabriel nor Joseph had aught to do with the formation of the Child; that was by the Spirit's power.‡

And some minister of God may come to us with the word of vocation, or some friend may be the guide of our spiritual life, but the Spirit of God alone can produce the life within. Remember it in your life, in the regard of all earthly instrumentality; the priest may be the holiest, the guide the wisest, the friend the dearest; they may help, but the utmost they can do is what Gabriel and Joseph did for Mary; the Spirit must communicate life.

* St John i. 12, 13.　　† Zech. iv. 6.　　‡ St. Luke i. 35.

And as in your life, so in your work; you can but do what Gabriel did and Joseph; you cannot create spiritual life in others ; you can guard it, you can bring this and that one under the influence of the Spirit of God; you can do as the bystanders did at the grave of Lazarus; you can remove the stone out of the way, in order that Jesus Christ may have the chance, so to speak, of getting at that soul. But He is the Resurrection of those who are spiritually dead as well as the Life of those who live.*

Don't try to impress *yourselves* too much on others; it is too much the tendency of human friendship. Do not try to play the part of human father to Jesus Christ in the soul; learn to stand by, and let the Spirit do His work. We are not so much to go before the human soul as to follow after it. We are not to seek to mould others according to our own pattern, but to render them mobile and plastic to the Spirit's dealing; encourage them to follow Christ, to be obedient and docile to His Word; that

* St. John xi. 39, 25, 26.

His likeness may be reproduced in them, as in us, by the operation of the Holy Spirit of God.

Think, then, of this Mystery of the Incarnation:

i. That we are made partakers of the Divine Nature.

ii. That the Divine Life is to be manifested in our life and in our circumstances.

iii. And that all this is to be by the Spirit's power.

"Oh!" you say, "this is something too high for me to rise to!" Remember Mary shrank and shuddered at the message; but the Angel said, "Fear not, Mary," for "the Holy Ghost shall come upon thee, and the power of the Highest shall overshadow thee."

Let us say Psalm ci.

SIXTH MEDITATION.

THE PURIFICATION OF THE VIRGIN MOTHER.

Let us meditate upon the Purification of the Blessed Virgin Mary.
Contemplate the Mother, standing in the Temple Court, holding her Child in her arms, waiting to offer Him to the Lord, and to present the offering for her purification.

O Almighty God, most Holy and most Merciful, purge us, we pray Thee, from all defilement of flesh and spirit, that we may worthily draw nigh to Thee in prayer and all the means of grace, and be more and more purged from evil; that so, as living members of the mystical Body of Thy dear Son, we may find acceptance with Thee now and at the last, for His sake in Whose Name we pray.

Our Father.

We have come to the consideration of

another Mystery of Joy, the last of the Joyful Mysteries; with a note of warning and prediction of coming woe in the words of Simeon—"a sword shall pierce through thy own soul also." *

It was a great day for Blessed Mary when she took her Child, God's own Son in our nature, to present Him, the offspring of her womb, to His Heavenly Father in the Temple; and when she too herself for the first time after His Birth and the accomplishment of the Angel's message, entered the courts of the Temple. We may be sure she sang her *Magnificat* over again, as her solemn thanksgiving for the great things God had done for her and in her.

I. Let us think of her now in the Purification, as giving us *an example of diligence and perseverance in God's worship, and in the use of the means of grace.*

The Law of Purification and Presentation did not strictly apply to her case and that of her Child. There was no need of purifi-

* St. Luke ii. 35.

cation in that Child-bearing; she had con-
tracted no stain; in that Birth there was
nothing in the least degree contrary to perfect purity, for He was "conceived by the
Holy Ghost, born of the Virgin Mary."
Nor was there any need of redemption in
His case; He was indeed Himself the Priest
and Victim, the First-born Son Who, by the
sacrifice of Himself, was to redeem all.
Neither was there any need in His case of
the Circumcision—the rite that was a badge
of sin, and told of the need of mortifying
unruly desires. In Him there was nothing
that swerved from perfect correspondence
with God's design. But no dispensation had
been given, so no exemption was claimed.

So it was with our Lord at His Baptism.
He came to Jordan with the rest to receive
that which was a sign of the washing away of
sin, in order that He might "fulfil all righteousness,"* not Himself to receive cleansing, but to sanctify water to the mystical
washing away of our sin. We have a simi-
lar example of this diligence in using the

* St. Matt. iii. 15.

means of grace in Mary's yearly visit to the
Temple. It was not of obligation on the
woman's part, as it was with men; but she
did not excuse herself, or urge the plea
that it was difficult to leave her Child at
home with the rough crowd at Nazareth, or
that there was no need for her to go up to
the Temple where the services were so per-
functorily performed; she was better em-
ployed at home with her Child! Ah! what
plausible reasons might have been urged!
but none were used. His parents went
yearly to the feast.* Blessed Mary gives us
an example of diligence, of faithfulness and
earnestness in seeking God in all appointed
means of grace.

Then let us examine *our* regularity in the
use of the means of grace—times of prayer,
sacraments, fasting-days, rules of self-
denial, and so on. And not only our diligence, but our *earnestness* in our use of
them; coming to the Sacraments with right
dispositions, with a real spiritual appetite,
with "hunger and thirst after righteous-

* St. Luke ii. 41.

ness." * Do we seek to excuse ourselves,
asking, "Need I?" "Must I?" This
surely is not a Christian question. A better would be, "*May* I?" "Is there any
means by which I may serve ⌐God better,
by which I may express more truly my
loving sorrow for past sin?" We are not
to serve in the spirit of bondage, but as
loving children in the spirit of adoption.†
Let us set before us Blessed Mary as an
example of diligence and earnestness in
approaching God, in the use of all the means
of grace.

II. *Consider the reward of this diligence
and faithfulness*, of which we have the
pledge and example in the Purification.
"Unknown" she is, "yet well-known." ‡
She goes up to the Temple like any other
mother, but she is recognized by Simeon
and Anna, and she receives a further confirmation of her faith in their recognition.
And they too had been purified by long
discipline and waiting, and now their faith-

* St. Matt. v. 6. † Rom. iii. 15. ‡ 2 Cor. vi. 9.

fulness is rewarded by the vision vouchsafed
to them. They had waited long years, looking for redemption in Jerusalem, and Simeon had received the promise that he should
not pass away till all was fulfilled, until he
had seen the Lord's Christ. There was so
much that was perfunctory in the Temple
rites; still they persevered, and lifted up
their hearts to God. And in the end they
are rewarded; Mary comes to the Temple,
and their spiritual vision is illumined.
Simeon sees that Mother, and in her Child
he recognizes the Lord's Christ, come to
redeem the world. It is the pure—the meek
—who "see God." * He takes Him up in
his arms and sings his *Nunc Dimittis*, and
blesses the parents. Ah! see the reward of
patient waiting on God.

Sometimes some of you are tempted to
give up attendance at Church, or at the
Sacraments, because the ministration is so
irreverent, or because so much is lacking.
"It is so little to my taste, I had better
absent myself altogether." No; if others

* St. Matt. v. 3.

are cold, go and be a centre of devotion
yourself; if others absent themselves, be the
more regular and earnest yourself; look
through the unworthiness of the minister to
Him Who is the Great High-Priest, Who
stands in the midst of the seven golden
candlesticks that symbolized the Universal
Church, Who holds in His Hand the seven
stars that represent the Priesthood of the
Church.* Look to Him for the reward of
your faithful attendance, your devout worship. "In every place" and rite "where I
record My Name, I will come unto you and
bless you." † And so in your own private
devotions. It may be your prayers are dull
and dead; your meditation is irksome—a
waste of time, it seems; you have no light.
Ah, but Simeon and Anna had waited a
long, long time before the Vision came at
last and repaid all their waiting; so "though
the vision tarry, wait for it; because it will
surely come, it will not tarry." ‡ God keeps
us waiting for the answer to our prayer
(not only for external benefits, but for spir-

* Rev. i. 13, 16, 20.   † Ex. xx. 24.   ‡ Hab. ii. 3.

itual graces also), not because He is grudging in His gifts, but because He would develop in us a greater capacity to receive.

So learn the lesson of faithful, patient, persevering diligence; and see the reward that in the end comes.

III. *Consider the reason of the delay on Blessed Mary's part in going up to the Temple.*

It was not until forty days were past, six weeks since the Birth of her Child, that she visits the Temple. Why not before? Bethlehem was but a little way from the Holy City.

She waited "until the days of her Purification were accomplishd." O how she longed meanwhile to go into the courts of the Lord! " O how amiable are Thy dwellings, Thou Lord of Hosts! My soul hath a desire and longing to enter into the courts of the Lord; my heart and my flesh rejoice in the living God!"* Have *we* such longings?—not merely to enter into the earthly

* Ps. lxxxiv. 1, 2.

sanctuary, but for some nearer approach to God in the spiritual life; to be able to speak more freely to Him in prayer; to hear His Word more clearly speaking in our conscience; to have our faith more clear and strong—those mists of doubt and temptation rolled away; to be free from that clinging temptation which is haunting us and dogging our path? Ah! but wait patiently "until the days of purification are accomplished," until the days of discipline are over; until a greater clearness of conscience and purity of heart may enable us to hear His Voice speaking to us.

Think of Mary's obedience to the Law concerning Purification, as laid down in Lev. xii., which subjected the mother after childbearing to a ceremonial cleansing from her defilement. All these provisions of the ceremonial Law are full of spiritual significance. They were intended as object lessons before the eyes of the people witnessing to the holiness of God and the need of holiness in approaching Him. Just as contact with a leper or with death communicated ritual defilement and needed ceremonial purification, so was it with the handing on of life. It was the handing on of a tainted, marred nature; not as God originally made it, but fallen and disordered. Therefore it involved defilement, and cleansing was required. The rites for purification after childbirth witnessed to original sin. Ah! we have need to remember that quite as much for our encouragement as for warning. We are not unfallen creatures in an unfallen world; it is not safe for us to use all the pleasures that are in themselves innocent. We have a natural tendency to sink down to earthly things; and the world, in its fallen condition, has a tendency to drag us down in our fallen condition; to act as a screen—shutting God out from our sight. There is therefore need of self-discipline, of self-denial in this and that particular, of keeping under the body, of losing the lower to gain the higher life.

And think what a lesson of comfort there is here! God knows all that; He knows the condition of our fallen nature, and He takes all into account. He knows its drift, how easily we go astray; how the flesh is weak even when the spirit is willing. We must come before Him in humble, penitent acknowledgment of our fallen estate, confessing and bewailing not only our sin but our *sinfulness.* "In sin hath my mother conceived me;" therefore, "make me a clean heart, O God, and renew a right spirit within me."*

Scripture expresses our experience. The lower nature wars against the higher; "the flesh lusteth against the spirit and the spirit against the flesh, so that ye cannot do the things that ye would." † "The good that I would, I do not; but the evil which I would not, that I do." "I see another law in my members, warring against the law of my mind, and bringing me into captivity to the law of sin which is in my members." ‡

I am sure that the distinction between "sin" and "sinfulness" is a very important and a very helpful one. So often a day passes, and we come to our self-examination

* Ps. li. 5, 10.   † Gal. v. 17.   ‡ Rom. vii. 19, 23.

at night, and we are not conscious of having committed any *sin* during the day. Then people get terribly frightened, and they think, "Dear me, what a state I must be in, to think I can have passed a day and not be able to find a sin!" But let us not disparage the work of the Holy Ghost. What is the use of the grace of God, if it is not to keep us from sin? What is Holy Communion for, but to keep us clean from sin? There ought to be many days on which we commit no definite sin of thought, or word, or deed. Perhaps we have had no special temptation. Or perhaps grace has been extremely powerful: you have felt it playing about you, you have been conscious of a higher power within. But notwithstanding this, we know that all has not been quite right within; there are the workings of evil there—of meanness, of jealousy, of self-indulgence; they have not come to a head, they have not been brought to a point, but they are there. "Though I have not sinned, I feel there has been the need of a strong hand to keep these workings of evil down. I know I carry about a sinful nature!"

So let us remember this distinction between " sin " and " sinfulness," and beg of God gradually to cleanse us from our sinfulness as well as from our sin.

This helps us to understand the distinction between the special cleansing given us in Absolution, and the cleansing power of the Body and Blood of Christ in Holy Communion. Absolution is especially for the doing away of sins. Where a sin has come in and clogged my spiritual life and hindered the free flow of regenerate life, absolution is the putting forth of a spiritual power to break down the barrier, and to cleanse away that which clogs the spiritual life. But Holy Communion—we are to come to that after repentance, with our sin forgiven and our conscience at ease, by our own drawing near to God and making our peace with Him, or, if need be, by special confession and priestly absolution. On the other hand, the Blessed Sacrament of the Altar is for the cleansing of our sinfulness, for the infusion of our

Lord's holy Nature to remedy all the defile-
ments of our fallen nature, "that our sinful
bodies may be made clean by His 'all-holy'
Body, and our 'sin-stained' souls washed
in His most precious Blood by the communication of His life."

Think how we may have to wait, like
Blessed Mary, for some nearer approach to
Him, some deeper sanctification of our
spiritual life, some fresh entrance into the
Temple of the Lord, until, at last, the days
of our purification are accomplished! Sometimes we are so lacking in patience and
humility—we want to die right off! We
don't know what need there is of purging
first, of cleansing within and without. We
have to wait for the resurrection of the body
and the entire rectifying of our nature to
usher in the life of the world to come; and
meanwhile we must use all the means of
grace at hand, all the sacraments, all the
disappointments and trials of life, all the
friction and vexations of life, that our earthliness and selfishness may be more and more
done away. And then, when all the discipline

of life is done, there is still the purification
of the intermediate state—the seeing ourselves as we are, as we see Him in His glory.
" I have heard of Thee by the hearing of the
ear, but now mine eye seeth Thee; where-
fore I abhor myself, and repent in dust and
ashes,"* in ever deepening penitence, until
at last in perfected penitence we find perfected purification, and enter the Temple of
the Lord to present the Christ-child formed
within us, in our life, our talents, our
gifts, our circumstances, by the Spirit's
power.

Once more, consider the spiritual significance of the special law of purification after
childbearing to which the Blessed Mother
was subject, as laid down in Levit. xii. We
find that in the case of purification after the
birth of a man-child (with which we are
alone concerned) there were these two
stages, symbolical of two stages of progress
in the spiritual life. First, for seven days
the mother was excluded from fellowship
with ordinary society. On the eighth day

* Job xlii. 5.

the mother entered on the second stage of her purification; she was restored to the company of her fellows, she was allowed to enter upon social intercourse; but still for thirty-three days more she was excluded from participation in the Temple rites; she could not yet enter the Temple of the Lord.

So, remember, there are stages of purification in our spiritual experience. There is a ceasing to do evil, then a learning to do well; a putting off of the old man and his deeds, and a putting on of the new man which after God is created in righteousness and true holiness.* There are two conversions of which St. Bernard speaks. He says that there is need of conversion *from the world to self;* like the prodigal son, who "came to himself" and found the world unsatisfying; and then there is the second conversion, *from self to God;* first we have to gain a true possession of ourselves, and then to use that possession in giving ourselves to God, losing sight of self in seeking

* Ephes. iv. 22–25.

the glory of God and the good of our brethren. So again we learn of the progressive stages of spiritual development. Don't hurry people, don't drive the flock too fast and hard, and don't be impatient with your own slow growth. And in the divisions of the days of purification we may find a spiritual signification. The seven days will represent the Old Testament dispensation—the purgative way, under the Law. Then, on the eighth day, when the Saving Name is given, that is closed. But there are thirty-three days more—a day for each year of the earthly life of the Incarnate Son, so making up the number forty, in Holy Scripture signifying the full number of probation and discipline. Yes, we are to follow the Lord in all the stages and departments of His life—in the hidden life at Nazareth; in His tempted life in the wilderness; in His social life with His disciples and His friends at Bethany; in His ministerial life, "going about doing good," spending and being spent for others; ever full of compassion for us in our needs, in toil for others, in works of mercy, corporal and spiritual; in His devotional life, in His nights of prayer, in His early mornings given to communion with His Heavenly Father, in His lifting up His eyes to Heaven in the midst of work, putting Himself in conscious communion with His Father. And then, likewise, in His suffering life. Ah! yes; to follow Him in each of those thirty-three days, in each stage and department of His life; to set Him before us in each department of *our* life, in our domestic life, in our devotional life, in all the experiences of sorrow and suffering that may befall us. Ah! Blessed Lord, grant that I may truly follow Thee step by step, as Thou dost present Thyself to me as my perfect example; day by day putting off the old man, and imitating Thee, becoming more and more conformed to Thy perfect likeness; in the purgative way and the illuminative way filling up the days of my purification, till in the unitive way I may present the fruit of grace formed within me, and in the Temple courts may sing *Magnificat* for the great things that Thou has accomplished.

"For He that is mighty hath magnified me, and holy is His Name!"

Let us say Psalm xxvi.

SEVENTH MEDITATION.

Let us meditate upon the Flight of the Holy Family into Egypt. Contemplate the vision beheld by St. John.* The woman clothed with the sun, with the moon under her feet, and having a crown of twelve stars upon her head; travailing in birth to bring forth the Man-Child which shall rule the world. And see over against her the monstrous beast, the great red dragon, standing before the woman, ready to devour her Child. And the dragon persecutes the woman and is wroth with her, and makes war with the remnant of her seed which keep the commandments of God and the testimony of Jesus Christ.

O Lord Jesus Christ, the Eternal Son of God, who wast in the world that was made

* Rev. xii.

by Thee, and the world knew Thee not;
who didst come to Thine own, and Thine
own received Thee not;* pardon, we beseech Thee, all our past resistance to Thy
grace, and grant that now henceforth we,
falling into rank beneath Thy banner, may
show ourselves Thy true servants and soldiers, ready to bear the opposition of the
world, the uprisings of our own fallen
nature, and the assaults of Satan, for Thy
Name's sake. Do Thou ever guard us
from evil, and overrule all contrary things
to our good, and enable us to serve
Thee faithfully, for Thy mercy's sake,
who livest and reignest with the Father
and the Holy Ghost, one God, world
without end. Amen.

Our Father.

The figure of the woman clothed with the
sun, and with the moon under her feet, and
having on her head the crown of twelve
stars, as beheld by St. John in his vision at
Patmos, and recorded in the 12th chapter

* St. John i. 10, 11.

of the Apocalypse, stands for the Church of God in every age, bringing forth Christ to the world. It has nothing whatever to do with the Blessed Mother in her present exaltation. It may be applied to her as the type of the Church collectively, and of every individual soul among the company of the faithful. She brings forth Christ personally; the Church is ever bringing forth Christ in the spirit. In every new planting of the Church in the mission-field, in every new religious movement, in every establishment of a guild or religious society, in every fresh individual resolve to live for Christ more faithfully—there is the bringing forth of Christ in some fresh manifestation of His grace and truth.

And over against that figure ever stands the great red dragon, the foe of Christ, ready to destroy the new birth of the Divine life.

So was it with Israel in Egypt; so was it with Christ born after the flesh; "Herod sought the young Child's life to destroy it."*

* St. Matt. ii. 13.

So was it with the infant Church; the Roman empire rose up to blot it out; and when Satan failed by persecution to destroy the seed, he sought to strangle it by heresy or to seduce the Church by worldliness. Ever over against the woman bringing forth the Man-Child stands the great red dragon, seeking to destroy His life. So it is in our own experience. We make some special resolution and we find some fresh obstacle. Some new start is made in mission-work; then fresh difficulties and hindrances arise. All this is quite natural; we are not to be in the least surprised or discouraged.

I. Consider, first, *the necessary antagonism that exists between the Church and the world, the woman and the dragon.* It is through the bruising of the heel of the woman's Seed that the serpent's head is to be crushed; it is only through struggle that Redemption is to be gained; it is only through suffering that victory can be effected.

And, as with the Church, so with the individual. Don't think that any opposition you may meet with in your life or in your work is any necessary sign of God's displeasure; rather it may be the reverse. Satan sees some germ of the Divine Life which, if it be allowed to grow, will work ruin to his kingdom, and he starts up to oppose it. Or the world scoffs and ridicules it. Yes; we are always to expect opposition; it is a sign of the Divine Life asserting itself in a fallen world. So, when He came into the world, when "the Word was made flesh," and "He came unto His own, and His own received Him not," Herod, as the representative of this world's power, sees his own throne tottering and seeks to destroy the new-born King. So it was with our Blessed Lord after His baptism. Mark the sequence of mysteries in our Lord's life. After His Baptism, when the heavens were opened above Him, the Spirit was seen descending and resting upon Him, and the voice of the Eternal Father was heard proclaiming, "This is My beloved Son;" then, immediately, "He is led into the wilderness to be tempted of the devil." * Before He enters on His ministry, before He works a single miracle, preaches a single sermon, or wins a single disciple, He will constitute Himself "a merciful and faithful High Priest;" "for, in that He Himself hath suffered, being tempted, He is able to succour them that are tempted." † He earns His right to teach and lead. Mark the Temptation before the Ministry, and the Temptation following right upon the Baptism.

There stands the Evil One. "Let us see what it means. *Art* Thou the Son of God? What means the proclamation? *Has* the Spirit descended on Him? It shall be wrested from Him!"

Ah! we are often discouraged because after receiving some grace some fiery trial assaults us. It is just the time to make the grace our own; as we act upon the grace given, the grace is appropriated and assimilated by us.

It was so, again, after the institution of the other great sacrament. Jesus leads

* St. Matt. iii. 4. † Heb. ii. 17, 18.

His disciples forth from the upper chamber of the Eucharist to share in His Passion, to the Gethsemane of spiritual wrest-
ling, the Gabbatha of contradiction, the
Golgotha of actual suffering and death. Ah!
if we would worthily show forth His death
in holy mysteries, we must in our lives be
conformed to His example.

So here Mary, who is brought so near to
Him, begins already to share His cup of
sorrows; the sword begins to pierce her
heart because she is the mother of Him who
is "the Man of Sorrows, and acquainted
with grief."* Think of Mary's sorrow when
the decree goes forth from Herod to destroy all the children of Bethlehem, in the
hope that among them may be her own
Child. That Child, as Simeon says, is set
"for the fall of many and for the rising of
others in Israel, and for a sign to be
spoken against."† Think of her sorrow,
not only for herself; *she* must share His
sorrow; but that, be sure, is not the first
thought in her heart. She sorrows for her

* Isaiah liii. 3.   * St. Luke ii. 34.

Child—that *His* interests should be jeopardized; she sorrows for all the mothers of Bethlehem; she sorrows for Herod, too; hating the sin, pitying the sinner. Ah! "many and great are the troubles of the righteous, but the Lord delivereth him out of all." *

Think then first of the necessary antagonism between the Church and the world, between Christ and Satan. The Child is born, and the enemy seeks to destroy its life. Be prepared for opposition; don't be surprised at difficulties in your life or in your work.

II. *Consider the example of Detachment;* for that is the lesson we learn from the Flight into Egypt. Think what was involved in it. Three months had passed since the birth in Bethlehem; the Magi had come from their distant homes; the Holy Family are now, comparatively, comfortably lodged at Bethlehem; the pressure for room caused by the taxing has passed away; they are no longer

* Ps. xxxiv. 19.

in the stable, the Magi found them in their house.* People, too, have become friendly, attracted by the unearthly sweetness of the Holy Family; their attention also had been aroused by the message of the shepherds, and by the coming of the Eastern travellers. Mary is now able to go to the Temple when she pleases; she is in comparative proximity to the Temple while at Bethlehem. And Mary at Bethlehem is in the home of her ancestors; she is of the line of David, his heiress.

It has been supposed by some that the very stable in which the Saviour was born belonged to the old homestead of David and Jesse; that the little town had grown up around it, and that then it was used as the caravansary of the place.

Mary is at home in Bethlehem, in a place full of sacred associations. And now all this is to be sacrificed. There comes the message to arise at once, and fly into Egypt—into *Egypt*, where, indeed, there is a considerable colony of Jews, and where they would be free

* St. Matt. ii. 11.

from Herod's jurisdiction and interference; but it is a heathen country, and associated in the minds of every patriotic Hebrew with the idea of bondage and of Israel's degradation.

Carry the Child *there*—to such a desolation? Oh, how strange are God's ways! "His ways are not our ways, nor His thoughts our thoughts." * He gives such strange, paradoxical commands, so contrary to what *we* should have thought! And they go. Ah! think of it.

Are *we* called tol eave some Bethlehem ? Are we despatched to some spiritual Egypt ? Are we called to give up some cherished attraction, some bosom companion, some helpful guide, and sent to some spiritual Egypt to carry our experiences to those who are less privileged than ourselves, to impart to them what God has given to us ? Or are we laid by through sickness, and compelled to give up some cherished work, not for ourselves, but for the good of others ? Are we disqualified by sickness, or by invalidism,

* Isaiah lv. 8.

which is worse? It is like being sent into
Egypt. Do we go like Mary, promptly,
carrying the child with us? Or are we in-
wardly rebellious, repining, discontented,
reluctant?

They go "with haste;" they pack up and
start at once. Egypt will not be the land of
desolation if God bids them go thither, and
if they carry the Child with them. Palestine
would be no " Holy Land," nor Bethlehem
"the house of bread," unless they were
there at God's bidding. "No, Lord, let
Egypt be my dwelling, at Thy command;
not the Holy Land with all its privileges,
nor Bethlehem, at my own self-will. Any-
where with Thee, O Lord; nowhere without
Thee!" "Lord, I will follow Thee whither-
soever Thou goest."* "In all places where
I record My Name, I will come unto thee
and I will bless thee;" † but at no altar which
thou hast devised and erected for thyself, for
thine own will-worship! Are we ready to
leave our spiritual privileges and blessings
when God in one way or another deprives us

* St. Luke ix. 27.   † Ex. xx. 24.

of them ? How often we have our perverted ideas of what means of grace and sacraments are to do for us ! We have an idea that all are to support us and to hedge us round; that, while we are weak and tottering, Almighty God will put a strong staff in our hand on which we may lean ! Almighty God will do nothing of the kind. He gives us His sacraments to be our food and strength, so that we may come to live by His *indwelling* might.

When from time to time, from one cause or another, we are debarred from the means of grace, then is the time to show what we have gained from them in the past; and that we have not merely enjoyed them, but profited by them.

Let us think, then, what a lesson of detachment Blessed Mary gives us, not from mere natural human associations, but from whatever God sees fit to withdraw from us.

III. *Consider the example of Obedience and its reward* that we have in the Flight of the Holy Family into Egypt.

We may note five points concerning it:

(i.) The security which comes from obedience.

Thus the young Child's life is saved. The Angel comes with the warning message, "Herod will seek the young Child's life to destroy it. Arise, flee into Egypt."‡ And Joseph obeys; he takes the young Child and His mother, and the life of Jesus is preserved.

Ah! how often an angel comes to us with a warning word—"they seek the young child's life!"—that young child of grace in the good resolution you made at the beginning of Advent, or at your Christmas Communion, or at the opening of the New Year, or in the resolve with which you leave your Retreat. "They seek the young child's life!" —the world, the flesh, the devil, your own besetting sin, your special temptation is lying in wait; avoid the occasion of evil!

How often have we neglected that warning voice which came to us in some inspiration—the word of a parent, the warning

‡ St. Matt. ii. 13.

of a friend, or the counsel of a spiritual guide! We were allowing ourselves some liberty; the voice said, "Beware!" We disregarded it, and the young child received some injury; maybe, it was killed outright.

Or, on the other hand, the warning came and we listened. "Beware of that evil, avoid that reading, that companionship, that amusement!" It was not in itself wrong, but for us it was seen to be dangerous. We looked back afterwards, and we saw what a danger we had escaped. And that other, who would not heed, fell into the danger and received a deadly injury. Learn the lesson of prompt obedience, to save the life of the child of grace.

(ii.) We have the example of *unconditional* obedience. "Go, flee into Egypt, and be thou there until I bring thee word again." Not for two months, or six, or twelve; not for two years or four. No time is specified, no term is given; but, "until I bring thee word again."

We must not make conditions with God; and yet we are always trying to do so. "I

can submit to *this*, but *that* I cannot stand!"
"I can take this sickness, but that disappointment I cannot bear!" "I can be put aside for *this* winter, but not beyond!"

Ah! there must be no making terms with God; the obedience must be unconditional. "Go. Be ready to *do*, to *be*, to *bear* what I order now, and then thou wilt be ready to do, to be, to bear whatever I have in store for thee in the future." Remember St. Jeanne Chantal's paraphrase of the Lord's Prayer: "Without 'if,' without 'but,' without exception, without limit, Thy will, O Lord, be done." Yes; "flee into Egypt, and be thou there until I bring thee word again."

(iii.) Then, again, consider how all this trouble came through the wickedness and violence of King Herod. It was that which rendered the Flight necessary. It was his envy, his fear, lest his own usurped sway should come to an end.

How often do we resent trials that come to us through the mistakes or the faults of others. We say, "If it came directly from the hand of God I could accept it." So we say, and so we think. "But it does not; it comes from the stupidity and perverseness of this or that person!" What did the Passion of our Lord Jesus Christ come from? Was it arranged by Heaven? It was all the work of *hell*—base, false, cruel. "This is your hour and the power of darkness,"* said our Lord; and yet, almost in the same breath, "The cup which *My Father* hath given Me, shall I not drink it?"† These two words of our Lord at His apprehension in the Garden represent the two aspects of all sorrow and all suffering. Regard it as the cup which the Lord gives, although it may be tendered by an evil hand. God allows many things that He does not inspire, and He will overrule for good all the evil that He allows, if only we will take it aright. "The cup which my Father gives," appeals to all the loving, trustful submission that is in me. "This is your hour and the power of darkness," appeals to all that is noble, strong, brave and generous in me. I will not be beaten; I will stand my ground!

* St. Luke xxii. 53.　　† St. John xviii. 11.

Think of this in any sickness, or misunderstanding, or opposition, any sorrow or suffering that may befall you; think of its twofold aspect, and how it is to be met in this twofold spirit.

(iv.) *Think of the example of obedience on the part of those set to rule.* It is the *parents* who obey, those who are in charge of the Holy Child. They have to show themselves obedient to the Heavenly Father whom they represent. None are fitted to rule unless they have first learned to obey. Oh, my friends, what a special lesson for any of us who are charged with the care of others! We have no right to rule unless we can submit ourselves as those under authority. Children are to obey their parents, pastors, teachers, "in the Lord;" but these must be in the strict line of representation; we must be obeying Him if we are requiring obedience from others in His Name; if we are ourselves lacking in obededience, we forfeit our right to rule.

See what a wonderful example of obedience is shown in the life and conduct of St. Joseph,

who was set to be the head of the Holy
Family, the guardian of the Blessed Mother,
the foster-father of the Holy Child. On
every occasion on which St. Joseph is mentioned in the Gospels, he is acting under
obedience.

(1.) Before our Lord's birth Joseph was in
sad perplexity as to the purity and faithfulness of his espoused wife. It was his duty,
according to the Levitical law framed to
guard the sanctity of family life, to put her
away. He was about to act in obedience to
the Levitical law, and, at the same time, to
obey the law of kindness in his own heart
which urged him to do it privately.*

(2.) The Angel comes and gives the explanation which sweeps away all his fears:
"That which is conceived in her is of the
Holy Ghost."† He bids him arise and take
unto him his wife, and give her shelter and
protection. Without hesitation he acts on
the Angel's word. In blind faith he accepts
the explanation. The world may scoff at
his simplicity, but "to the pure all things

* St. Matt. i. 19.   † St. Matt. i. 20.

are pure;"* and the loving and the generous can believe in the faithfulness of others.
He takes her and shelters her.

(3.) They go to Bethlehem at the command of Cæsar, for the taxing.† He obeys
not only the Angel, he obeys God through
whatever channel the command comes.
The heathen emperor is the civil ruler, and
in his sphere he represents Almighty God.

(4.) The child is circumcised on the
eighth day according to the Law; and the
Saving Name foretold is given by Joseph in
faith,‡ as the Angel had bidden.

(5.) On the fortieth day the mother is purified and the Child presented and redeemed. §

(6.) And now at the bidding of the Angel
he takes the young Child and His mother
and flees into Egypt, and waits there until
the Angel comes to tell them that "they are
dead which sought the young Child's life."

(7.) Then in obedience "he returns into the
land of Israel."

(8.) As he returns, when he hears that

* Titus i. 15.   † St. Luke ii. 1–4.
‡ St. Matt. i. 21.   § St. Luke ii. 21–25.

Archelaus, the cruel son of his cruel father, reigns in Judea, and he is afraid to go thither, in obedience to the Angel's word in a dream, he turns aside to Nazareth.*

(9.) And afterwards, year by year, he is seen attending the Temple feast at Jerusalem, until at last the Child is initiated in the Law.† And then his work is done, and he passes away; the Holy Child needs no longer his guardianship. "Guided by His counsel," He will, at last, "receive him into glory."‡ And after a little while that Son whom he had guarded and tended, shall come and claim him in Paradise.

Thus on every occasion Joseph is seen acting in obedience to the command of God, however expressed, whether directly by inspiration, or by the word of an Angel, or through the ecclesiastical or the civil law. As one who is set to govern, he is fitted to rule by unhesitating, unconditional obedience.

(v.) One last word. *When we obey God's*

* St. Luke ii. 22, 23.   † St. Luke ii. 41, 42.
‡ Ps. lxxiii. 23.

word, "*all things work together for good.*" *

All seemed so unlikely, so contrary, but all is taken into account by Almighty God. All is foreseen and arranged for. By St. Joseph's obedience not only is the Child's life spared, but the old prophecy sees its fulfilment, "Out of Egypt have I called My Son.† He turns aside to Nazareth at the Angel's bidding, because it is unsafe to dwell where Archelaus reigns, and another saying of the prophet is fulfilled, "He shall be called a Nazarene."‡

Ah! the things that seem so untoward, that are due to people's sins and Satan's wrath, God will make them all "work together for good;" all sorrows, trials and temptations, yes, and even our *falls*, if repented of. "All things work together for good to them that love God." "His wisdom reacheth from one end to another; mightily and sweetly doth it order all things."§

Let us repeat Psalm lxiii.

* Rom. viii. 28.　† St. Matt. ii. 15; Hosea xi. 1.
‡ St. Matt. ii. 23.　§ Wisdom viii. 1.

EIGHTH MEDITATION.

THE LOSING AND FINDING OF THE HOLY CHILD IN THE TEMPLE.

LET us meditate upon Mary losing and finding the Holy Child in the Temple.

Consider her remonstrance, as she finds Him after the three days' search. " Son, why has Thou thus dealt with us ? Behold, Thy father and I have sought Thee sorrowing." *

O Lord Jesus Christ, deal with us, we pray Thee, in Thy love and wisdom, as Thou seest to be best for us. Train us by Thy discipline; enable us to grow in Thy knowledge and Thy love; remove from us all that is displeasing in Thy sight; kindle in us true devotion, and an earnest desire to serve Thee. And grant that when the trial and discipline of life is over, we may behold Thee

* St. Luke ii. 48.

in the Heavenly Temple, and in Thy presence may find the fulness of joy. To whom, with the Father and the Holy Ghost, be all honour and glory, world without end. Amen.

Our Father.

We find Mary again in the Temple some twelve years after we beheld her there at her Purification. She then presented her infant Child to the Lord. Now He accompanies her, a Boy of twelve years old; and we have to consider a mingled mystery of joy and sorrow. She has a joy almost greater than any she has yet experienced, and a sorrow certainly not less. She had fled from Bethlehem *with* Him to preserve His life; now for a while she has to mourn the loss of Him. During twelve years she had been at the Temple feast; hitherto she had left Him at home, now He accompanies her. He has come of age to be initiated into the Temple rites, to take His part in its ceremonies; He has become a Child of the Law. Think what joy is hers as she takes her Boy in that caravan of pilgrims from Bethlehem to Jerusalem!

Some of you, perhaps, have experienced a like joy when you have taken your child, or a pupil, or a godchild, to Confirmation or to First Communion. Think of Mary and *her* Child, and what joy and pride swelled her heart! Think of the new meaning that came to her in that psalm, when she said, " I was glad when they said unto me, *we* will go into the house of the Lord. *Our* feet shall stand in thy gates, O Jerusalem!"* Think how she knelt by His side in the Temple courts; how they had looked forward to that day, talked about it, and about the Temple rites. And now they see them all enacted. Think of the questions He asks, and of her explanations. Think of His voice, as it rings out clear among the voices of the Levites, as they chant David's Psalms. How they seem to gain new meaning as He utters them! As when a master-musician takes the instrument into his hands, and we never knew what sounds it could give forth before; so

* Ps. cxxii. 1.

the Psalter, on the lips of the Son of Man, rises to a fulness of tone, gains a richness of harmony never known before in the Temple worship.

Think of Mary's joy at His devotion, at His wisdom, at the questions He asked when being catechized, as it were, by the scribes and lawyers in the Temple court. We are not to think of our Lord as sitting down to teach the doctors—such an idea would be altogether preposterous! The doctors sat round in a semi-circle, the pupils sat at their feet, hearing them and asking them questions. But the questions *He* asked suggested meanings such as they had never known; He was giving far more information than He received; they were amazed, and His mother was astonished too; there was an outshining of wisdom in her Boy such as she had not seen before. So think of her joy.

But remember that *we* can pray along with our Lord Jesus Christ in a better and more intimate way than was even granted to His Blessed Mother in the Temple. We are incorporated into His mystical Body. His

Spirit has communicated to us "the mind of Christ." Not until after Pentecost could she pray "in His Name." We pray not *alongside* of Him, but *with* Him, as an indwelling Inspirer. Ah! think of what our prayer should be in the sanctuary, praying along with Christ, as members of Christ, and with the aid of His Spirit. Think what it means —*to pray in Christ's Name*. It does not mean just to tack on Christ's Name at the end of a prayer, as a sort of charm; as though the weak petition that bubbles out of our heart could gain acceptance if so offered in His Name! No; to pray in Christ's Name means to pray with Christ's authority; it means to have Christ praying in us; we praying the prayers He prays—praying under the inspiration of our Head. Our prayer is not simply to pass through His Hands, to find an echo in His sacred Heart. No, no; it must be originated in His Heart, and then echoed by us. What does *He* desire for me? I must beg from Him the Spirit of grace and of supplication, that I, who know not what to pray for, nor how to ask as I ought, may be helped by the Spirit of Christ, that I may think His thoughts, have His desires, and pray along with Him.* Think of this in your private prayers. Think of the reverence and attention that should characterize prayers which are offered along with Christ's inter-cession. Think of yourself as kneeling on one of the lower steps of the Altar Throne on which He pleads on our behalf, gathering up all the prayers that are prayed by His faithful servants on earth and in Paradise. Think of the spirituality that should mark the prayers of Christ's members, who pray along with Him.

Again, think of prayer at the Holy Eucharist. He joined in prayer and Mary joined with Him, assisting at the Temple sacrifice. We are privileged to join in offer-ing the Sacrifice which is the antitype of all the Jewish sacrifices. The Eucharist is the earthly counterpart of the Heavenly pleading. We contend that the Holy Euchar-ist is the great central act of devotion, that it is the only divinely appointed service of

* St. John xvi. 23, 24; Rom. viii. 26.

the Christian Church; that nothing must be
allowed to take its place, whatever may be
the most convenient arrangement of services.
But we so often make a mistake here.
The Holy Eucharist is not our great act of
worship, because in it we plead and offer
Christ as our *substitute.* He is not our
substitute, He is our great Leader and
Representative. He did not die that we
might not die; He did not suffer that we
might lead a self-indulgent, luxurious life!
We must arm ourselves with His mind.* He
does for us that which, without Him, we
could never have attempted, but in which
we must share if we would be partakers of
the benefits of His life and death. It is
not His death as our substitute that we
plead. We gather round about Him, and
He leads our devotions. As we show forth
His "obedience unto death,"† in His own
appointed way; as we plead

> The only offering perfect in Thine eyes,
> The one, true, pure, immortal sacrifice,

we must "offer and present ourselves,

* 1 St. Pet. iv. 1.   † Phil. ii. 8.

our souls and bodies" along with Him, as our reasonable service to the Father. It is His *obedience* that God delights in, not His *death*. God delights not in death; not in mine, or yours, or His dear Son's; but in *obedience*. It is the willingness to suffer in God's cause unto death, the "obedience unto death," with which God is well pleased. That is the offering we show forth in glad thanksgiving and exultation, and at the same time proclaim as the law of life for ourselves to follow, in the Eucharistic mystery.

Ah! think what our Eucharists involve. There the Head gathers the members about Him; He offers them along with Himself, and the Church offers herself along with Him, the great Head, the Representative of the Christian Society. As we gather round our Leader and assist in the presentation of Him who is both Priest and Victim, He makes us, likewise, "kings and priests unto God and His Father." *

But if we go forth from our Eucharists to

* Rev. i. 6.

live idle, self-indulgent, self-pleasing lives, think, what are our Eucharists but our condemnation? This is what we plead; this is what God delights in—Christ's *obedience unto death*, and we rule the straight, clear line of His obedience, only to make more plain the crookedness of our own want of correspondence with His will!

Think, then, of Mary joining with Him in that worship of the Temple; and let us think of ourselves joining with Him in better fashion in the great Sacrament of the Eucharist.

Think again, how Mary in that Temple worship gained a new realization of her Son's character and personal dignity.

And think how we, year after year, festival after festival, Retreat after Retreat, are to grow in the knowledge and love of God, and of the things of God; keeping the old ways, not just in the old fashion, but diving down to a deeper significance, rising higher through fresh inspiration; not recurring to them as mere historical events, but as sources of real spiritual power. My Bible reading, my spiritual exercises, my Confessions, my Communions, my Retreats—all are to help me grow in the knowledge and love of God. Am I seeking to gain a newer and truer conception of the things of God, in nature, in providence, in grace? Are my heart and my understanding kindled with a new knowledge and love of God? Am I seeking to attain a child*like* spirit, while I put away child*ish* things? There is all the difference in the world between being *childlike* and *childish!* We are to "*put away* childish things,"* childish conceptions of prayer, of God, of the sacraments, of our Christian life; while we retain a childlike spirit of trust and love. All this is difficult. There must be humility, patience, trustfulness and love, if we are to grow in grace. But we are, remember, to offer to God the homage of our *mental* faculties; we are not to let them grow in secular knowledge, while they remain stagnant and undeveloped as regards the worthiest of all acquirements—the knowledge of spiritual things.

* 1 Cor. xiii. 11.

Think, then, of Mary accompanying her
Son, joining in His prayer, assisting with
Him in offering the Temple sacrifice, gain-
ing fresh conception of His character, His
dignity, and of all spiritual things along with
Him.

II. *Then think of the sudden change—the
sorrowful side of the mystery of that visit to
the Temple.* Yes; she experiences now a
sorrow greater than that of the reproach of
Nazareth, or the anxiety of Bethlehem, or
the flight into Egypt. All that was borne
with Him, now there is the loss of Him !

Ah ! be prepared for changes of experience in the spiritual life. The *Magnificat*,
which was the last recorded utterance of
Blessed Mary, is followed by this loving, sorrowful expostulation; the major key sinks
down to its plaintive minor: " Son, why hast
Thou thus dealt with us ?"

So it is in our life! There is a time of
joy, of festival joy, of spiritual joy in
Retreat, when the things of God are so plain
and clear that we almost seem to see them,

to lay hold of them; it seems almost absurd not to live under their control; the supernatural seems the common sense view.

Then a cloud comes and settles down over us, and we wonder whether it could all have been true. That state of ecstasy—was it mere emotion, the effect of the imagination, or of some fascinating companionship?

Yes, there are all sorts of vicissitudes in spiritual as in natural circumstances, and many causes contribute to them. We must be prepared for them just as much as we are for changes of climate. Our *Magnificat* will often sink down to the plaintive expostulation with the Lord—"Why hast Thou thus dealt with us?"

It is worth noticing the sequence of sayings of the Blessed Mother. There are just seven in the Gospels, which mark out, as it were, the experiences of the spiritual life.

(i.) There is the word of *prudence*. "How shall this be?"* asked, as we have seen, not in doubt, but as testing the spirit, rightly

* St. Luke i. 34.

seeking to be assured that the message came from God.

(ii.) Then, so assured, there comes the answer of simple *self-surrender.* "Behold the handmaid of the Lord; be it unto me according to thy word." *

(iii.) Then, mark, she went to salute St. Elizabeth with the word of *loving kindness* and of sympathy. † Her great dignity did not make her stand on her rights, or wait for Elizabeth to visit her. Her great joy made her full of loving-kindness. "He that loveth God loveth his brother also." ‡

(iv.) Then comes her central saying, in which she pours out her whole soul to God in the *Magnificat.*§

(v.) Then follows this word—the word of *loving remonstrance,* telling of trials in the spiritual life. "Why hast Thou thus dealt with us?" ‖ Then follow the two other sayings, at the marriage at Cana of Galilee, which we shall consider later.

---

* St. Luke i. 38.   † St. Luke i. 40.
‡ I St. John iv. 21.   § St. Luke i. 46–56.
‖ St. Luke ii. 48.

(vi.) One, the word of *loving intercession*, bringing the needs of her friends before our Lord, seeing their difficulty and embarrassment. Her own sorrows had made her sympathetic; she is quick and eager to relieve others. "They have no wine!"*

(vii.) The other, as she retires from the scene as her Son enters on His public work, her word of *counsel*—"Whatsoever He saith unto you, do it."†

Look for something corresponding to this in your own life.

Now the festival is over; the company are returning to Nazareth; the caravan starts; and through some mistake the Child has not been informed; they start without Him. In the great company they suppose Him to be with friends and are not alarmed. But the night comes, they bivouac; and now they find Him not. They search for Him among their friends, and He is not there. Think of the agony of that night and how hastily they retrace their steps to the Holy City the next morning. All that **day**

* St. John ii. 3.　　† St. John ii. 5.

they search for Him; another night passes and they find Him not; not until the third day do they discover Him in the Temple.

O think of the sorrow of that three days' search! And is there not something of reproof in our Lord's answer to His mother's words: "How is it that ye sought Me? Wist ye not that I must be about My Father's business?" Or, rather—"*in my Father's house*"—for that, without doubt, is the correct translation. "How is it that ye sought Me? What did you go to the lodgings for? Why did you seek Me in the streets or in friends' houses? Why did you not come to the Temple? You left Me here, and here I am!"

Ah! and so it is continually in our own experience. It is not the Lord who has withdrawn from us, but we from Him. We cannot always have spiritual fervour. Maybe our natural powers have given out—the strain was too great. Or maybe our spiritual powers have given out; some temptation came and we gave way to it, we grew lax in self-discipline, careless in our prayers; we were not faithful to the inspirations of conscience; we have withdrawn from Him. And then we ask our Lord, "Why hast Thou thus dealt with us?" And He answers, "Here I am; I was waiting to hear your prayer, to feed you with My word, to give you Myself in the sacrament. 'Return unto Me, and I will return unto you.'* It is *you* who have changed; it is you who went away from My presence; it is you who deserted My holy Temple. Or, you sought to distract yourself in earthly pleasures and companionship, and you have failed! Ah! come back to Me, and find in Me the joy and strength of your spiritual life!"

We are not to be surprised at such experiences, nor to be discouraged by them. God tries His chosen servants. He would lead Mary and Joseph to value their treasure more highly, since they have been without Him those three days. Oh, how careful would they be afterwards, not to let Him out of their sight, that there should be no more mis-

* Mal. iii. 7.

understanding, but all quite plain and clear.

And when we have no sensible consolation, when all our spiritual exercises seem dry and dull, all mere forms, and we hardly know how to drag ourselves along in our spiritual life, He would have us cling to Him more closely, since we know how barren and dry a thing life is without Him. "Like as the hart desireth the water-brooks, so longeth my soul after Thee, O God."*

So think of Mary's joy and sorrow as the type and pattern of your spiritual experience.

III. Was there not some sense of failure on Joseph's part, of neglected responsibility? Ought he to have lost sight of the Holy Child? Ought he to have started without ascertaining that He was in the company, to have trusted to the chance of finding Him? Think of the remorse of St. Joseph. Mary might have chidden him: "It was your part to keep watch over the Boy; you are His

* Ps. xlii. 1.

appointed guardian!" And how he must have chidden himself for his thoughtlessness and carelessness.

Think of that as a sort of typical warning for any of us who are put in charge of the spiritual life of others, when through our neglect or carelessness, or inconsistency or bad example, we lose hold of them—the child committed to the parent's care, the soul committed to the priest's guidance and pastoral ministrations, the pupil to the teacher, the god-child to the sponsor—and we have forgotten them, or been careless, self-pleasing, neglectful. "Where is the flock I committed to thee?"

Think of Joseph's remorse, and of our own self-accusation; and learn the lesson of real carefulness, of earnest fidelity in the discharge of any such trust. Pray that you may never, by carelessness or bad example, put a stumbling-block in the way of a soul for whom Christ died.

Think of our Lord's words in that great High-Priestly prayer to His Father in which He reviews His life and ministry. "I have glorified Thee on the earth." * How? By success? It was, to all appearances, a ghastly failure! No; but because "I have finished the work which Thou gavest me to do." Never mind success or failure; outward success may be real spiritual failure; and outward failure, if we have been true and faithful, is not failure in the sight of God. "I have manifested Thy Name unto the men whom Thou gavest Me out of the world; Thine they were and Thou gavest them Me "—those few—that little handful! "Of them have I lost none."

And those people He has given Me; those few placed under my influence—can I say "of them whom Thou gavest me have I lost none, but the son of perdition?"† There was that limit to the success of Jesus Christ. He could not, He would not force Judas. He will woo, and attract, and allure, but not compel. And there is that limit to *our* influence; we cannot force any against their will.

But let us live so as to be able to echo our

* St. John xvii. 4.   † St. John xvii. 12.

Lord's words, " Of them whom Thou gavest
Me have I lost none"—by carelessness, by
want of energy, or by bad example.

And let us learn the same lesson as regards
our own life. We have failed. It has been
our own fault; we see it. Our life has
grown dull, our faith is less bright, our love
less active, and our hope has become clouded
over. We have withdrawn from Him; we
have not been careful to obey His inspirations. "I looked for my beloved, but my
beloved had withdrawn himself and was
gone . . . I sought him but I could not find
him; I called, but he gave me no answer."*
I am punished for my own faithlessness.
Then, "I found Him. . . I held Him and
would not let Him go."† I will be more
careful, more faithful in my spiritual exercises, in my self-examination, in avoiding
occasions of evil; more true in all my duties. He has chastised me; I have learned
" how evil and bitter a thing it is to forsake
the Lord."‡ " But He has not dealt with me
after my sins, nor rewarded me according to

* Cant. v. 6.   † Cant. iii. 4.   ‡ Jer. ii. 19.

my iniquities."* "Heaviness may endure
for a night, but joy cometh in the morning."† "Then shall ye call upon Me, . . .
and I will hearken unto you. And ye shall
seek Me, and find Me, when ye shall
search for Me with all your heart."‡

Let us repeat Psalm xxx.

* Ps. ciii. 10.   † Ps. xxx. 5.   ‡ Jer. xxix. 12, 13.

NINTH MEDITATION.

THE VIRGIN MOTHER AT THE MARRIAGE
FEAST IN CANA.

Let us meditate on the example of Blessed Mary at the Marriage Feast of Cana. Listen to her word of intercession, as she brings the needs of the company before our Lord, and says, "they have no wine."* And hear her word of counsel to the servants, "Whatsoever He saith unto you, do it."†

O Almighty God, who hast ordained and constituted the services of men and of angels in a wonderful order, and hast incorporated us one with another in the mystical body of Thy dear Son; grant us, we beseech Thee, ever the spirit of loving fellowship, that we may rejoice with them that do rejoice and weep with them that weep, that so, bearing

* St. John ii. 3. † St. John ii. 5.

one another's burdens here, we may be fitted to have our share in the company of Thy saints above, through the same Jesus Christ our Lord.   Amen.

Our Father.

Eighteen more years have passed since the last events recorded in the life of the Blessed Virgin Mary; and meanwhile, so far as the Gospel record is concerned, she has been left in silence, pondering over the things she has seen and heard.*

Now again we have a mystery of mingled joy and sorrow; as if here on earth we were to expect no unclouded happiness, as if our brightest joys were to be dashed with streaks of pain.   The Child has developed into the Boy, the Boy has become the Man, and the Man has entered on His public work.   We turn from the narrative of St. Luke, which tells of the Infancy of our Lord (gathered probably from the Blessed Mother herself), to the story of St. John.

And, you will remember, the marriage

* St. Luke ii. 19, 51.

feast at Cana was the occasion of St. John's introduction to St. Mary, who from the Cross was made his sacred charge.

Think what the intercourse between that Mother and her Son must have been during those years at Nazareth. How He had grown up in her presence, and she had advanced in the spiritual life under His eye! We see them now together at the marriage feast.

I. *Consider the example which the Blessed Mother gives us of sympathy with both the joys and the sorrows of others.* She was fitted for this by her own experience. Her own deeper experience did not crowd out the thought of others; she had learned to feel for others because she had felt so much herself. Think of Mary's presence at the marriage feast as the expression of her loving interest in other's joys. She can enter into their joys, although she has put aside all ordinary wedding joys for herself. Perhaps the bride was some friend—her sister, or her cousin, Mary the wife of Cleophas? It mat-

ters not; she is invited, she goes. She does
not say, "All this is too earthly, too low
for me!" She accepts the invitation and
goes to the wedding-feast. She takes an
interest in it, she adds to their innocent joy,
and cares for their distress when the supply
of wine becomes exhausted.

Ah! think of this; as we become more
spiritual, let us take care not to become awk-
ward, odd or unnatural. We do such harm
to religion in this way! If, in our family,
or in society, or in our work, or with our
pupils, others cannot look to us for sympathy,
then they are repelled from the religion we
profess. Surely, the religion of Jesus Christ
should make us *more* truly men and women!
We may have to renounce something that is
less good for something that is better, but
don't let us try to impose this sacrifice upon
others. Don't say, "You must give up
going to the theatre because I find it better
not to go." Don't be strait-laced with your
pupils or your scholars; be large-hearted.
Don't be above sympathizing with their
interests. You may have more refinement,

culture, and higher interests than they have; but these are things that interest them. Keep them from harm, but don't frown on what is harmless, or else they will say, "We will throw off all religion!"

There is a grand saying which I have never been able to trace beyond a sermon of Dr. Liddon's: "The real Christian should have a heart of *steel* towards self, a heart of *fire* towards God, and a heart of *flesh* towards his neighbor." All these should go together. Sometimes we forget this and reverse their order, especially in the earlier stages of spiritual development. We forget the heart of flesh, and because we are strict with ourselves, we become hard with others. Or maybe there is the heart of steel towards our neighbor, and no heart of fire towards God, and a heart of very tender flesh towards ourselves and our own indulgences. No, no; if we are really strict with ourselves, we shall have the heart of flesh for others; just because we know how difficult it is to keep straight ourselves, we shall be ready to condone with others; and we shall be able to sympathize with others because we have learnt by experience our own frailties.

Do not with your brothers or with friends, be hard and repellent; let your religion make you more considerate, more loving and attractive, more able to think of and enter into the pleasures and interests of others.

Think of Mary, the mother of the Eternal Son, at the marriage feast, bringing joy and brightness, shedding an atmosphere of sweetness and purity all around her.

Think of her sympathy with the *distress* of those who have bidden her to the Feast. She recognizes their need. The scanty household store, which was all that their humble circumstances could afford, has been exhausted, possibly by the unexpected arrival of Jesus and His disciples. With a true woman's instinct she sees their embarrassment and enters into their distress. She does not say, "Let them feel their earthly need; it will make them appreciate the heavenly better!" She goes to her Son, who also sees the need, and, what is more, relieves it.

Do not smile at what people call "mere philanthropy." Try to raise it to something better. Do not hold in contempt what is done for others, because it is not always done in the best way. It may, perhaps, help them to embrace religion and fit them to receive spiritual truths. How can you expect the starving and naked to rise up to the desire for heavenly things? "That is not first which is spiritual," says St. Paul, "but that which is natural."* Our Lord Himself when teaching by parables begins with things earthly—with what is close at hand; and then He says that all these things have a meaning deeper and higher. He takes the earthly and says, "Now learn from that—from the needs of your body—the need that your *souls* have of refreshing!" You learn from your duty to your earthly parent your duty to your Heavenly Father. What is the child's first idea of God, but of some one higher, wiser and better than the wisest, greatest, best person it knows—its parent! Think of that. A child will gain its first

* 1 Cor. xv. 46.

idea of God from its earthly parent, who either demands its obedience as a tyrant—"defy me if you dare!"—or who lovingly trains it and supplies its needs in a better way than it can ask, and who guards it and leads it on to better things.

So think of Mary, seeing the temporal need of her friends, and setting herself to relieve their anxieties.

Are *we* stirred by the sense of others' need? Think of that word of hers—"They have no wine!" Oh, how it should echo from our heart and lips in prayer! There is not only the absolute poverty of life, but the *joylessness* of so many; not only of those whom we ordinarily speak of as "the miserable classes," but the joylessness of so many in the world—of the rich and the worldly. They have money, and they don't know how to spend it; they have possessions and pleasures, and they don't know how to use them; they have no real happiness in their lives—"they have no wine!" Oh, how we should try to win them by love, to bring their needs before our Lord, to try in every way we can, by our influence, our example, our words of exhortation, to bring joy into others' lives. And there are those who are less fortunate than ourselves. How we should use all the gifts that have been bestowed upon us for the common good. Your educational advantages, your refinement, your culture, your knowledge of literature, your musical talents, your art—what are they for? Simply to make money by? God forbid! To distinguish you from others? No gift was ever bestowed in order that the one to whom it was given might be separated from others by that gift! No; it is to be a link to bind us together. "I can do something that my brother cannot, therefore he has a claim on me, and I will stand by him." We are made to be necessary to one another; and for all the gifts we have, as trustees for the common good, we are responsible not only to Him who has given them, but to our companions and our fellow-men also *for* whom He has given them.

Think. Are we using the advantages

that God has given us in trust, for our
brethren—our scholars?

Mary *interceded*. Ah! she does so now,
for those who have no joy, no brightness in
their lives; for those who don't know Him.
And we must intercede along with her. If
we join in her song of praise in the *Magnificat*, we must unite in her intercessions also,
and bring the needs of others before our
Lord; and as we bring them, do all we can
to supply them. "Give *us* this day our
daily bread," not, "Give *me mine!*" The
Lord's Prayer is not said in the singular,
but in the plural. "*Meum*" and "*tuum*"
are not Christian words; "*Pater noster*" is
the Christian prayer and the law of Christian
life and conduct. What we value for ourselves we must seek to spread to others;
and what we shrink from ourselves—lower-
ing surroundings, a tainted atmosphere—
what we shrink to think of those nearest and
dearest to us being exposed to—let us do all
we can to remove from others. "Lead *us*
not into temptation. Deliver *us* from evil."
Do what you can to sweeten the mental and

moral atmosphere that surrounds you, my sisters. All can bring others' needs before our Blessed Lord; and then, like Mary, leave Him to supply them as He sees best.

Then let us go on to Mary's *word of exhortation*. She not only prays, she speaks to the servants her one recorded word of exhortation—"Whatsoever He saith unto you, do it." See what should be the word of a teacher. Not, as we saw before, trying to impress *yourself* on others, but to render them plastic to *His* inspirations, in order that Christ may impress Himself upon them by His Word, by His Spirit, in their conscience. "Whatsoever *He* saith unto you, do it." Whenever we have the opportunity, let us give the word of exhortation and advice. Do not let us be overcome by shyness or false shame, but speak the word in season. Like the Blessed Mother, point to Him; only, like Blessed Mary let the word of counsel be the echo of your own conduct. "*Whatsoever* He saith unto you"—even though it be to fill the pots with water when it is wine that is wanted—"do it." *She* could say that because she had done it herself. Her word of exhortation is the echo of her own word of self-surrender in response to the Angelic message, giving herself up in simple faith, "Behold the handmaid of the Lord; be it unto me according to thy word."* "How shall I be carried through? How shall this word be accomplished? How shall I be protected?"—She did not know, nor did she very much care. God had spoken; He would be true to His word. And "all things spoken by the Angel concerning the Virgin Mary were accomplished." Out of her own experience she could give the word of counsel, "*Whatsoever He saith unto you, do it.*"

Ah! if only our words could be seen to be the outcome of our own experience, then they would have real force. But if we are only seeing very plainly what others ought to do, while *they* see very plainly that we are not doing what *we* ought to do, then we had better not speak at all. Mary is calling

* St. Luke i. 38.

others to that saintly life in which she seeks to abide.

So consider the example of Mary's sympathy at the marriage feast, seeing their need, and setting herself to relieve it by her intercession and her counsel.

II. *Consider Mary's sorrow and discipline at Cana.* The scene is one of changed relationships. It is the first time that Mother and Son have met since He left her at Nazareth to enter upon His ministerial life. Oh! think of what her sorrow was as He told her He must go; that those days of loving intercourse were over, that He is going to leave Nazareth, to leave *her;* that the Father's business required it.

Then followed the Baptism, the solemn inauguration to His Ministry by the forerunner. Then came the forty days' fast, and His fierce struggle with the Evil One. Then the return from the wilderness, when John had pointed Him out to his disciples as the new Teacher:—" Behold the Lamb of God, which taketh away the sins of the world!" * and handed over to Him some of his own pupils whom he had been training for the Christ—Peter and Andrew, James and John, Philip and Nathaniel—these had been called to be the Lord's disciples.

And now the Mother and Son meet again. Jesus goes with those disciples to Cana. She sees a change in Him. His bodily frame is wasted with His forty days' fast; His face is lined with the marks of His terrific struggle with the Evil One; she has a foreboding of what is to follow. They are never again to be together as they were before. He has new interests now; His disciples are His first thought; they are His intimate companions; they have taken her place!

Ah! think of the sacrifices *we* are called to make as our friends go from us, or as we are called to leave them. I sometimes think that those who are left behind make quite as great a sacrifice as those who go; as the priest, the missionary, the religious, or any who are called to live a life of separation; and, if so, if they share in the sacrifice,

* St. John i. 29.

then, be sure, they share in the blessing too.
When that friend or that pupil is called to
something beyond you—to something to
which you are not called, ah! then think of
the sacrifice that Jesus made, and that Mary
made when she sent forth her Son.

. Then, think of the check to her natural
feelings. She sees Him with the first-fruits
of His disciples, and she rejoices that He has
such enthusiastic friends; the mother's heart
was stirred, of course,—for she was a true
woman. They tell her about His baptism,
of which John had told them; of the Spirit
descending like a dove and resting upon
Him; and of the Father's voice proclaiming,
"This is My beloved Son."* They tell her,
too, of the Baptist's words, "Behold the
Lamb of God, which taketh away the sins of
the world,"—how he had been preparing the
way for the Messianic King, and had pointed
Jesus out as the Expected One. Her heart
is on fire! Do not think me disrespectful—
she has a natural ambition (St. Chrysostom
says so); she would have her Son to be a

* St. Matt. iii.

King, and she would share His throne!
And now she would have Him work a miracle. This gives the key to His answer.
There is nothing disrespectful, nothing
rough, in the reply of Jesus: "Woman," or
as we might say, "Lady" [the word is constantly so rendered in the Greek plays]
"what have I to do with thee?" But there
is an insistance upon a changed relationship—
"What is there in common between you and
Me in this matter? In my private life I was
subject to you, as a son to his mother; now
I have entered upon My public ministry; I
am about My Father's business; and that
must be done, not in accordance with any
partial love, or dictates of natural affection."
He severs Himself from her jurisdiction by
this word. And how lovingly she takes it!
She turns to the servants and refers all to
Him. She points to Him, not to herself:
"Whatsoever *He* saith unto you, do it!"

Ah! and how often has our Lord dealt
thus with us. He sends us some check;—
our heart is set on the accomplishment
of some plan, some scheme which prom-

ises success; not for ourselves only, but for others—and God sends us a check. We cannot, as we look back upon it, deny that there was a good deal of self-love mixed up in it; it was *our* plan, and we were going to have a share in it; it was going to be a credit to us! And our Lord makes that plan fail; some one else carries it out. Ah! we must be purged from all self-love. So long as God's will is done and souls are helped, what matter whether the work be done by us or by others, in our fashion or in another; whether we gain credit and success, or discredit and disappointment? No matter, so long as the work is done. They have the wine of gladness, and it matters not whether we hold the bottle, or the servants; or whether the work be done in our lifetime, or by others whom He will raise up. We must rise above all petty and personal considerations, and we must expect our Lord to send checks in our life and in our work.

III. *Consider our Lord's example at the Marriage Feast of Cana, in His dealings with His Blessed Mother; His perfect Detachment and perfect Impartiality.*

(i.) *His Detachment.* He will not anticipate the hour which the Father has fixed: "Mine hour is not yet come."* He will not be moved by any mere partial love. "Who is My Mother, and who are My brethren?"† He will not respond to any merely natural claim. So must we make all natural claims subordinate to the heavenly; yet we must love all very, very tenderly. Do not think that love is lessened because it is controlled. No, no; it is strengthened, because all that makes it weak and vacillating is purged away. Strong love is pure. Love Him above all, and all in Him. "Whom have I in heaven but Thee? and there is none upon earth that I desire in comparison of Thee."‡ All others, however tenderly I may love them, are as nothing in comparison of Thee! So in all matters of life learn to put aside *preference*, while you stand fast by *principle*. We must distinguish our duty from our pleasure. It is very easy to call

* St. John ii. 4.   † St. Matt. xii. 48–50.   ‡ Ps. lxxiii. 24.

preference principle; but as we are ready to sacrifice our preferences, we can stand the more firmly by principle; and others will then learn to respect the principle to which we feel bound to adhere.

(ii.) *Our Lord's Impartiality*. He spares not His Mother, because she is so dear to Him. No; heroic souls are dealt with in heroic fashion. Because she is so dear to Him He cannot bear that there should be in her the slightest flaw or imperfection; she must be wholly conformed to the Divine will.

So if God disciplines us, it is because He loves us. "Whom the Lord loveth He chasteneth, and scourgeth every son whom He receiveth." * It is because He loves our best and highest interests. It is because He is so faithful in His friendship that He must warn us against the things that mar our highest perfection. Just so did our Lord deal with His disciples; that was why He was so severe with the chosen three whom He had admitted into the inner circle of His

* Heb. xii. 6.

friendship, and allowed to be with Him on certain special occasions; for instance, at the raising to life again of Jairus' daughter, at the Transfiguration, and at the Agony in the Garden. They were specially honoured, specially loved, and specially disciplined. How stern our Lord was with St. Peter! After his great confession, "Thou art the Christ, the Son of the Living God!" when he had drawn forth from the Lord an expression of joy—"Blessed art thou, Simon Barjona!—My work has not been in vain; thou hast learnt the truth I have been trying to teach My disciples, and hast won thy place, to be first among My Apostles and a foundation-stone of My Church!"—a little while after, when Jesus foretells His Passion and St. Peter would dissuade Him from it, our Lord turns to him with these words, "Get thee behind Me, Satan, thou art an offence unto Me; for thou savourest not the things that be of God, but those that be of men."* He does not say, "Peter has said so many good things, I must pass this by!" Not so.

* St. Matt. xvi. 13–24.

Because Peter had risen to such a height, he cannot be allowed to sink down to a low level. Because he had risen to the apprehension of spiritual things, he cannot be allowed to speak the things of earth.

And so was it with the fiery spirit of James and John; it must be regulated. They would call down fire from heaven on the Samaritans who would not receive their Master;* He sternly rebukes them, "Ye know not what manner of spirit ye are of!" "None of your Old Testament spirit of vengeance here! I want not the spirit of Elijah! Rise up to *My* spirit. The Son of Man is come not to destroy men's lives, but to save them. See the manner of My victory, conquering through love, winning through meekness, through self-sacrifice." Yes, His disciples must be disciplined and purged. His special friends must be treated with special discipline.

Let us expect our Lord to deal thus with us, as a faithful friend, and let us submit ourselves to His loving severity, His prudent

* St. Luke ix. 54.

training, even though He use the surgeon's knife. "Try me, O God, and seek the ground of my heart; prove me and examine my thoughts."*

And we will try to imitate His faithfulness, His impartiality in dealing with friends. We are not true to our friends if we are afraid of giving them pain. There are times when we ought to risk giving pain, and not to shrink from it. We must be ready to give pain if we love with real love; we must love so truly as to be willing even to be suspected at the moment of *not* loving. We must be faithful in our friendships, not letting ourselves be dragged down by our companions from the high standard to which God is calling us. In some instances we have seen, on our knees, quite plainly how we ought to behave under trying circumstances; for instance, in some misunderstanding, or when things are going wrong; in church matters perhaps, or in our own family; we see it all and realize how we ought to act, regarding it as an opportunity of showing meekness and

* Ps. cxxxix. 23.

patience of overcoming evil with good. And then some one suggests a different line, and we allow the suggestion to stir up all our bad feelings—"You can't let *that* pass! You can't allow yourself to be treated like *that!*— what will come next?" And so we retaliate, instead of being true to our conviction. Instead of insisting, as Jesus did, that His friend should rise up to His standard, we sink down to the lower level suggested by a friend, and so fail in loyalty to our God, and also to our friend! This was our opportunity for bearing witness to what God had shown to us.

So consider our Lord's example of faithfulness, and impartiality, and detachment.

Let us learn with Blessed Mary to sympathize with others' sorrows and with others joys, and to set ourselves with real active sympathy and earnest zeal to supply their needs. Let us seek like her to subject ourselves to our Lord's loving training and discipline; and let us strive to be true and faithful to all because we love Him, and because we love them truly and really, in and for God.

Let us repeat Psalm cxli.

TENTH MEDITATION.

THE VIRGIN MOTHER AT THE CROSS.

LET us meditate on the Blessed Mother standing by the Cross of our Lord Jesus Christ.

Behold her as beheld by Jesus; and listen to His word as He commends His Mother to the loving care of St. John, the beloved disciple, and says, "Woman, behold thy son!" and to St. John, "Behold thy mother!" *

O' Lord Jesus Christ, King of Saints, Who dost bind us in a blessed fellowship one with another as Thy disciples and as members of Thy mystical Body, grant us, we pray Thee, that loving Thee with a pure love, we may love all others whom Thou dost love, in Thee and for Thee. Grant us to use all the gifts Thou hast bestowed upon us, in nature

* St. John xix. 26, 27.

and in grace, for the good of the brethren, that so we may be numbered with Thy Saints, both now and evermore. Amen.

Our Father.

And now the Blessed Mother's cup of sorrow is full. We gaze on the climax of her woe, but only to remember that that depth of woe shall lead to a higher, more glorious joy than any she had yet experienced. From the Joyful Mysteries we pass on to the Sorrowful; and the Sorrowful Mysteries are, in their turn, to give place to the Glorious and Triumphant Mysteries.

But as she now stands at the foot of the Cross, all else is swallowed up in the contemplation of that fearful sight. We sing of her as standing by the Cross of her Son, but it is much too solemn and awful a thought for mere sentiment. We behold an illustration of the law of God's dealing with all His Saints, with all whom He calls near to Himself; and those who have a special share in His Son's exaltation must have a peculiar share in His suffering. It is the warning of the Old Testament; "My son, if thou come to serve the Lord, prepare thy soul for temptation."* And the warning of the Old Testament is taken up and transfigured in the Apostolic hymn of the New Testament, "if we suffer with Him we shall reign with Him."† It is the experience of His Saints. As James and John came and asked for high places in His Kingdom, He puts to them the test, " Are ye able to drink of the cup that I shall drink of ?"‡ As St. Bernard says, "What a shame"—and we might add, what an impossibility—"to be the soft and luxurious member of a Head that was crowned with thorns!" So does Christ bring to the Cross of suffering her whom He loved with a peculiar love.

> By the Cross, her station keeping,
> Stands the Mother mournful weeping,
>   Where He hangs, the dying Lord.
> For her soul, of joy bereaved,
> Bowed with anguish, deeply grieved,
>   Feels the sharp and piercing sword.

Ah! think of her sorrow! "For a mother to be present at the death of a child, an only

* Eccles. ii. 1.   † 2 Tim. ii. 12.   ‡ St. Matt. xx. 22.

son, and that mother a widow, is an affecting thought at any time, a grief too deep and mysterious for any perhaps quite to understand but those who have felt it. But for *that* Mother of *that* Son to stand by and see Him condemned to death as a malefactor, crucified between robbers, reviled and insulted, to hear Him cry, ' My God, My God, why hast Thou forsaken Me?'* and to be unable to minister to Him, *this* surely is a secret and mystery of anguish as much above what ordinary mothers can understand as their grief is more than can be comprehended by any but mothers." † Hagar sat a good way off and cried, "Let me not see the child die!" ‡ But Mary stands by the Cross and sees the death of her Son. She does not shriek, or faint, or fall down; she *stands* there in a majesty of sorrow, "perplexed, but not in despair; cast down, but not destroyed." § She shares her Son's lot.

I. *Consider her standing by the Cross as we*

* St. Matt. xxvii. 46. † Isaac Williams.
‡ Gen. xxi. 16. § 2 Cor. iv. 8, 9.

have seen her all through her life, as the representative of the Church, the type and figure of the faithful. Ah! is she *my* pattern, standing by the Cross? The Cross is set up in my life, in my family life—do I bravely stand by it? In some bereavement, or in a painful misunderstanding, do I stand, like the Blessed Mother, overwhelmed, maybe, with grief and shame, yet still looking up to God, not in bitterness, but believing? Or is the Cross in our work? Some failure comes, or disappointment, or pecuniary anxiety, do we stand by that Cross? Or it is in our own personal, individual life; temptations assail us, a dark cloud settles down on our soul, spiritual difficulties arise— do we give up then? Or are we found faithful? Do we stand by the Master? Or, the Passion is renewed in the Church's experience; there are anomalies, difficulties, heresies. But troubles do not call for fretfulness and impatience; the Church is to be tried, like her Head; she is to share her Lord's humiliation. She is to be like her Master, "unknown" to earth, "yet well-known" to Heaven;* "crucified through weakness, yet living by the power of God." † Am I faithful to principlè, yet humble and forbearing, not bitter or complaining? Am I standing, like the Blessed Mother, *patient* by the cross, not seeking to be rid of it? Am I standing by her in *sympathy*, seeing *Him* suffering in the poor, the sinful and the ignorant—ministering to Him in them? "Inasmuch as ye did it unto one of the least of these My brethren, ye did it unto Me!" ‡ Am I standing there in readiness to bear His lot, ready to share His scorn and shame? And am I standing there in *worship*, beholding the glory of the Cross, the moral beauty of the sacrifice, not in mere admiration or idle sentiment, but rendering the true homage of imitation?

Is not Mary learning a deeper lesson than before? Surely, as she stands by the Cross, she is gaining, as all through her life, a further revelation of her Son's character, His dignity, His work, His kingdom. The Old Testament Scriptures—the Levitical sacri-

* 2 Cor. vi. 9. † 2 Cor. xiii. 4. ‡ St. Matt. xxv. 40.

fices, the prophetic types of the Passion—
now she has the key to many things that had
puzzled her.   Now she learns that the suffering Messiah is to be the triumphant Messiah;
that He is to reign in meekness, to conquer
through suffering.   The Apostles had not
learned before the true characteristics of His
kingdom; they had dreamed of an earthly
kingdom, and Mary had shared their
thoughts; it would have been impossible
for her to be altogether free from them.
Now she learns the truth, she learns in what
His true dignity consists; she dies with Him
to every earthly hope, every mere natural
ambition.   The Cross was to her, as to all
who were to be incorporated into the humanity of her Son, the key of heaven, the door-
way to a better life.

Think.   Are we ready, like Mary, to stand
by the Cross, in worship, in readiness to learn
its mysteries, to set ourselves to follow in our
Lord's steps ?

II. *Think of Mary by the Cross, recognized
by our Lord Jesus Christ.*

" Now there stood by the Cross of Jesus His

Mother, and His mother's sister, Mary the wife of Cleophas, and Mary Magdalene. When Jesus therefore saw His mother, and the disciple standing by, whom He loved, He saith unto His mother, Woman, behold thy son! Then saith He to the disciple, Behold thy mother!"*

He saw her from the Cross. Ah! think of what He saw as He looked around! He beheld the soldiers—rough, brutal, ignorant—with their wine, their dice and their spoils. He beheld the chief priests mocking in their malice, exulting that at last their plan had succeeded, they had got rid of their rival. He saw the penitent robber; He turned to look at him, to accept his confession, and to give him His word of promise. He looked for St. Peter, but St. Peter was not there. He had said he was ready to go with Him to prison and to death, but he had denied Him, and now we may suppose he was ashamed to return and stand by Him. He saw that little band of disciples, mostly women, of all classes, under the guardianship and patronage of St. John. There was Magdalene, the

* St. John xix. 25–27.

penitent; Salome, the matron; and the Virgin Mother.

Ah! as the Cross is continually reared throughout the ages He looks to see if those whom He has called to be His disciples are standing there. Does He see *us* standing, in faithful love and courage, by His Cross?

See Him faithful in the fulfilment of filial duty to the very end. He had separated Himself from His Mother at His Father's call. But when, on entering upon His Ministry at the Father's call, He subordinated earthly ties to Divine obligations. He did not cease to *love;* He did not obliterate His earthly love; human love is only made more pure, more strong, more enduring by subordination to Divine love. Therefore when there was no conflict of claims, His last thought was for His Mother, as He seeks to provide for her, and commends her to the loving care of the disciple whom He could trust.

A Son that never did amiss,
That never shamed His Mother's kiss,
Nor crossed her fondest prayer :

E'en from the tree He deigned to bow
For her His agonized brow,
  Her, His sole earthly care.*

Who, O perfect filial heart,
E'er did Thee a true son's part,
  Endearing, firm, serene ?

See in this the consecration of all natural
ties, the re-hallowing by the Cross of all
family affections and kinship.   Have all your
natural relationships been re-hallowed by the
Cross of Jesus—re-hallowed at the beginning
of a New Year by the cradle of Mary's Child,
by Him who became a member, not merely
of *the* human race, but of *a* human family;
who became your Brother to enable you to
fulfil all the duties of your family and social
life, with love, with purity, with peace ?

III. Consider *the creation of new relationships around the Cross of our Lord Jesus
Christ.*   Mary and John, the mother and the
friend of Jesus, are given to one another in
a new way, to be something more to one another than they had ever been before.   John
is to play a son's part to the bereaved mother,

* Christian Year.

and the mother is to look to him for guidance, protection and support, while she gives
to him comfort, sympathy and love. Think
of the new relationship, the kinship of grace
that was formed around the Cross of Jesus.
Think of Mary as the representative of
the Church, and John, whom Jesus loved,
as the type of the individual among the faithful. Or of John, as the representative of the
priesthood, and Mary as the elect soul com-
mended to the care of the ministry. Or see
in them two chosen souls, loved by Jesus,
drawn nearer to one another as they are
drawn near to Him and to His Cross. See
here your relationship to the Church, to the
ministry, to your fellows. Learn to be all you
can to one another. Think of being given to
one another by Jesus from the Cross. O the
tender love, the respectful ministry we should
exercise one towards another! Think of Mary
receiving John at the Cross, and of John receiving Mary. Think of that friend, that
pupil, that soul whom you can help, support
and cheer, as given you by Christ from the
Cross: "Take this child and nurse it for

Me," He says.* Ah, take all your interests, all your duties, all your charges *from* the Lord; care for all *for* Him, love all *in* Him, and then give back, with purity of intention, all *to* Him.

Think of this new alliance between Mary and John, how it is to be reproduced continually in the family of the faithful. Learn what we should be to one another, each to each; Mary giving comfort, as woman can to man, and John giving protection and support, as man to the Blessed Mother. Think of the converse of those elect souls; think of Mary, giving him cognizance of facts in the early life of Jesus which she alone could know; and of John giving her deeper insight into the meaning of those facts—that her Child was the very Word of God, of one nature with the Father, "by whom all things were made;" that it was *He* who was made Flesh of her substance, "full of grace and truth."†

Think how we should supplement each other's knowledge, be large-hearted, wel-

* Ex. ii. 9.　　† St. John i. 14.

coming different views of truth, so long as they do not contradict one another—balancing and supplementing one another. Remember that truth is infinite, and our minds are very finite. Do not seek to make others see only what you can see; then how very little any would see ! Don't merely *tolerate* —no one wants to be tolerated, it always implies superiority on the part of the one who tolerates ; but generously *welcome* another's view, it will supplement your own and make it richer, fuller. Learn largeheartedness by the Cross of Jesus Christ.

IV. Pass on to consider now *Mary's share in the Glorious Mystery of the Resurrection.* She is not mentioned in the story of the Resurrection; and that is just the point. She is not mentioned all through the story! The last we see of her is at the foot of the Cross, when the Lord commends her to the care of the beloved disciple ; then she vanishes from our sight in the Gospel records. Legend has been busy, and Art has stepped in where it has no sanction. In art she is represented as assisting at the entombment; and legend tells the touching story of the Lord appearing first to His Blessed Mother on Easter morning. But how much more grand is the simple statement of the Evangelist: "He appeared *first* to Mary Magdalene!"* Blessed Mary needed no such assurance of His Resurrection. She had stood by His Cross, and she knew He would triumph. She knew that *that* was not the end, that God's promise could not end in failure, that He would not leave His soul in Hades, nor allow His body to see corruption;† that somehow or other death would be overthrown and the victory won; that His words would be fulfilled, that He would "rise again."‡ She had stood there at the Cross, "steadfast in faith, joyful through hope, rooted in charity."§ So she is not at the tomb. Nor is she there on Easter morning with the women, to pay, as they thought, the last act of homage to their dead Master, and to embalm the corpse. What was that

* St. Mark xvi. 9.   † Ps. xvi. 10.
‡ St. Matt. xx. 19.   § Baptismal Office.

to her? He is not going to lie in the grave; she will stay at home till word is brought to her that Jesus lives, that He has conquered Death, that He has dispersed His foes! Others may mourn their Master, but she knows that her Son and Lord will triumph. So she needs not a sensible appearance.

To whom did our Lord vouchsafe a special appearance ? Not to the great saints, but to the penitents; not to John who stood at the Cross, but to Peter who had denied Him; not to the Virgin Mother, but to the Magdalene; to Thomas, who could not believe; to the two disciples who were straying off discouraged to Emmaus;. to the weak who needed special strength; not to the whole, but to the sick.

Ah! don't expect all to be sweetness, comfort, sunshine, because you are seeking the Lord; rather, the absence of sensible comfort may be a token of advancing strength. The little child is carried in its mother's arms, but as it grows it is put down that it may learn to walk, and stand by its own effort. We are not always to be carried, like children, in the arms of grace; we are to learn to stand and to walk.

So think of our Lord's dealings with His Blessed Mother in the days of the Resurrection, and that the absence of any sensible appearance to her was a token of greater spirituality, of stronger spiritual vision, on her part.

And learn, likewise, the lesson of *impartiality* from His dealings with His disciples —how He shows Himself, not to those, if we may say so, to whom it would have been the greatest pleasure to appear; not to John, His bosom friend, not to His Blessed Mother, but to Peter who had denied Him; to the Magdalene who was weeping at the tomb, and fearing lest the terrible cloud which the presence of the Master had driven away should take possession of her again. She had felt safe in His presence—what was to become of her now? And so she weeps bitter tears at His grave. He must go and comfort her, and tell her that though gone from sight, He would be evermore near to guard and protect her. "I am not come to call the righteous, but sinners to repentance." *

And He would have us act in the same way, with the same purity of intention, concerning our friends and those who have been committed to our care. Not to do what we should most *like*, to seek those whom it would give us the greatest pleasure to be with, but those who *need* us most, who most require our care.

Think of that lesson of impartiality and contrast it with our own practice. There is this or that girl or child who takes in everything that is said—you can almost see the lesson taking root; she is so appreciative, it is a delight to teach her; you give *her* lots of time, you write to her from all parts of the world! And there is that other, so dull, so lacking in responsiveness, surrounded by such unfortunate circumstances, in such danger—she is so hard to get on with, so difficult to get at, so encrusted with the hard shell of reserve! This one needs all the greater care; the other is sure to get on; this one re-

* St. Matt. ix. 13.

quires all your prayers, your thoughts, your loving sympathy. Yes; Jesus went to Mary Magdalene, to Peter, and did not vouchsafe a special appearance to the beloved disciple or His Blessed Mother. Learn the lesson of really acting in His Name, of taking your charge from Him, loving it for Him, and then offering it to Him.

i. So think of Mary standing by the Cross in her sorrow, sharing her Son's shame and suffering, as the pattern of the faithful soul.

ii. Think of her as seen by Jesus, and spoken to by Him from the Cross; and of the hallowing of all natural relationships. Think of the creation of new ties and bonds of grace by His Cross as He gives Mary and John to stand in a new relationship to one another.

iii. Consider on the day of Resurrection, the absence of Mary's name in the story—not to her discredit, but rather to her honor, because she can do without that special manifestation; she is not dependent upon sensible help; her faith is stronger, her vision clearer.

iv. Think of our Lord's impartiality as giving us a law for the discharge of all duties we seek to fulfil in His Name, and for His sake.

Let us repeat Psalm lvii.

CONCLUDING ADDRESS.

THE VIRGIN MOTHER WAITING FOR THE GIFT OF THE HOLY GHOST.

WE have thought all through the Retreat of the example of the Blessed Virgin Mother as the type and figure of the Church collectively and of each individual soul in the company of the faithful. We have dwelt on every instance in which she comes before us in the Gospel narrative, and on her complete surrender to the will of God. We have thought of her predestination, of her genealogy, of her training in her early years, of the light thrown upon her previous history by her words at the Annunciation; we have thought of the Angel coming to her at the Annunciation, of the accomplishment of God's great purpose concerning her. We have dwelt on the Visitation, and on the mutual joy of the Blessed Virgin and St. Elizabeth, and on the outburst of that joy

as she breaks forth into her glad *Magnificat*.
Then on the Birth of the Lord and the accomplishment of the Mystery that had been
foretold. Then there was the Presentation
in the Temple and the Purification of the
Mother. We passed on to consider the Sorrowful Mysteries: The flight into Egypt; the
loss of the Child and her words and His on
the finding in the Temple; the mingled
mystery of joy and sorrow at the marriage at
Cana of Galilee. And then we thought of her
presence at the Cross and of the significance
of the absence of her name from the story of
the Resurrection.

There is just one other occasion, and one
only, on which her name is mentioned in the
New Testament. In Acts i. 14 we find her
waiting with the Apostles in the upper chamber for the day of Pentecost. The faithful
eleven were gathered together in the upper
room where the Lord had celebrated the first
Eucharist, and had told them of the promised
Comforter. There they had gathered together on Easter Day, and there the news had
been brought to them, " The Lord is risen

indeed!"* There He had appeared to them on the day of the Resurrection, and again on Low Sunday. There, after His Ascension, they are keeping their Retreat, and "continuing with one accord in prayer and supplication with the women, *and Mary the Mother of Jesus*, and with His brethren.' They are waiting for the fulfilment of the promise which they had heard of Him.

The last time we see her she is on her knees in prayer, the type of the Church and of every faithful soul. She has done her work; now she is on her knees in prayer, looking for fuller gifts, not for herself alone, but for others also. Thus we part with her, not as a mediatrix—not prayed *to*—not prayed *through*—but prayed *with;* there is the company of the saints, and Mary in the midst; all are brethren and sisters, praying together in the Body of Christ. See her waiting there, praying with them for further gifts—for the Gift of the Holy Spirit, beyond what even *she* has received before.

* St. Luke xxiv. 34.

I. Ah! think how, in going out of Retreat, you are to go in the spirit of prayer; your last thoughts to be on your knees before God, thanking Him for all He has said and done for you, and looking for some further gifts. Yes, in Retreat spiritual things seem so clear and vivid, so real. We know that the shock will be great on going out into the world; it is like going out of a hot house on a cold raw morning ; we get a chill, and spiritual cold may be quite as fatal as physical; it may fly, not to the head, but to the heart.

We have to cherish the spirit of our Retreat, and to cherish the retreat exercises all through our ordinary life; in our home anxieties, our social distractions, in all the pressure of our ordinary work and occupations. We are to be, like Blessed Mary, on our knees in prayer, thanking God for all He has given us. "Mary kept all these things and pondered them in her heart." *

II. *Think of her as the true Woman*—the ideal both of the matron and the maid—the

* St. Luke ii. 19.

Blessed Mother on her knees in prayer. The apostles and disciples go forth to their labours, but think of that blessed home where she and John are together. Think how it must have cheered the hearts of the others to know that John was offering the Holy Eucharist, and Mary assisting at it, pleading for them and for the success of their preaching. Think of their coming back, one by one, and being cheered by the loving care of the Blessed Mother and the beloved disciple. Think of the great apostle St. Paul with all his wondrous powers, being introduced to her. Think of what woman's work should be!—not her mere active work, but that other side of it, her *influence*. Praise God for it. Try to support those who have not the same opportunities for prayer that you have; and let others be gladdened by your intercessions. And let your work be strengthened and tranquillized by the inner devotional side of your life. *Don't let work crowd out prayer.* Think of the blessings brought down on the Church through the intercessions of the Blessed Mother and St. John.

III. Once more. *Blessed Mary was wait-ing with the Apostles and Disciples for a fur-ther Gift of the Holy Ghost.*

The Spirit at the Incarnation had over-shadowed her; but that was an external work. He had, indeed, taken of her sub-stance to fashion the sacred flesh in which the Eternal Son was to live and die and reign; but now she is looking for something more. That holy manhood had been disci-plined and sanctified by His life on earth, "perfected through suffering," until in the fullness of glory He should sit down at the Father's right hand, thence to send His Spirit on His Church. And now His Spirit is to take of the things of Christ and to give them to Mary! Now, Mary is to be partaker of Christ's substance. He had taken hers; the Spirit had come upon her at the Annun-ciation; now, that which she had given is to be given back to her, and that glorified human Body is to interpenetrate her very being; she is to be admitted to a closer union with her Lord—far, far closer than that which she had enjoyed during those nine months between the Annunciation and His Birth. Now He dwells in her heart, now she is to be made- partaker of His glorified humanity.

And so think that whatever gifts we *have* received, there are further gifts in store. Whatever light we *have* received, there is a still clearer illumination awaiting us. Onward and upward! " Forgetting those things which are behind, and reaching forth into those which are before "—pressing on, year after year, retreat after retreat, through all the varied experience and discipline of life— that we may attain "the mark of the prize of our high calling of God in Christ Jesus," * that we may lay hold of that for which we are laid hold of by God;"

To Whom be glory for ever. Amen.

* Phil. iii. 13, 14.

APPENDIX.

THE VIRGIN BIRTH.

No APOLOGY can be needed for venturing to
discuss this subject. The question in these
days is forced upon us:

(I.) On what grounds do you believe the
miraculous conception of Christ? (II.) Is
it possible—or reasonable? (III.) What is
the moral value of the doctrine? These are
the chief forms in which the question is presented to us. Let me offer a few suggestions
with regard to each of these points.

I. Stress is laid on the fact that the miraculous conception is told only by two out of
the four Evangelists; that the story takes
somewhat different forms in the two Gospels
in which it is found; that St. Mark's Gospel,
which is supposed to represent the earliest
record of our Lord's life, is silent on the

subject; that nothing is said about it in the remaining books of the New Testament.

As Dr. Abbott puts it, "Of the nine authors or thereabouts of the different books of the New Testament, only two contain any account, reference or allusion to the miraculous conception." *

Such is the objection, or adverse argument, so far as Scriptural testimony is concerned.

To this reply may be made:

(1.) That the point was not one on which the Apostles in their early teaching would be likely to dwell much. Their special function was to be *witnesses* of what they had seen and heard. Accordingly they insist chiefly and continually upon the actual truth of the Resurrection of their Master—a miracle, which, being themselves absolutely assured of its truth, they urged as at once (*a*) the sign and the vindication of Jesus' Messianic claims, and (*b*) a manifestation of the superhuman dignity of His Person. "Born of the seed of David according to

* *The Kernel and the Husk*, p. 267.

the flesh, He was declared to be the Son of God with power, according to the Spirit of holiness, by the resurrection from the dead." *

This preternatural fact, the fulfilment of the "sign" which He had Himself promised,† a fact concerning the reality of which they offered themselves as witnesses,‡ would carry with it a readiness to accept a fact like the Virgin-Birth concerning which the same sort of evidence was not possible—a defect, it may be remarked, which it shares with the paternity of every child of Adam.

(2.) The silence of the Fourth Gospel on the subject is certainly no difficulty. For, on any theory of its date or authorship,§ it is a supplementary record, and with few exceptions does not reiterate statements of historical fact, which had already been related by earlier Evangelists, and which were by

---

* Rom. i. 3, 4.

† St. John ii. 18 sq.; St. Matt. xii. 38 sq.

‡ Acts i. 22; ii. 32, etc.

§ I beg that this expression may not be understood as implying any doubt on the writer's part as to the Johannine authorship of the Fourth Gospel.

the time this Gospel was written a part of the commonly received belief of the Christian Society. Bearing this in mind, and the general character of St. John's writings, it would seem rash to say that there is "no allusion" to the Virgin-Birth in the Fourth Gospel. The description in the prologue of the spiritual birth of the faithful, "which were born not of blood, nor of the will of the flesh, nor of the will of man, but of God "—in close connection with the statement that "the Word was made flesh"—would seem to suggest, very probably at any rate, a parallelism in the Apostle's mind between the spiritual birth of those to whom the Only-begotten Son gave the privilege of becoming sons of God, and His own Birth in our nature.*

In any case St. John's account of the Incarnation in no way conflicts with the miraculous story related by St. Matthew and St. Luke. Rather, as we may see later, his teaching concerning the Person of the Incarnate *Logos* is felt to be a natural

* St. John i. 12–14.

explanation of what might otherwise have seemed in them to be fantastic.

So with regard to St. Mark. Had he given any account of our Lord's early years, there would be some ground for pitting him (so to speak) against St. Matthew and St. Luke. But his story begins with the Baptism as the inauguration of Jesus for His public ministry—quite naturally, if the tradition be true (which there seems no reason for doubting, while there is a good deal of internal evidence in its favor) that Mark's Gospel is practically the putting in writing of Peter's oral teaching. St. Peter begins his account of the Lord's life ("the beginning of the Gospel of Jesus the Christ, the Son of God") at the point where he came in contact with the Christ, handed on to him by John the Baptist."*

(3.) But St. Matthew and St. Luke, it is said, give different accounts of the miraculous conception. We have " two Annunciations," one to Joseph and one to Mary. What of that? Does it not show—as, in a

* Comp. with St. Mark i., St. John i. 29 sq.

somewhat different way, the varying accounts of the appearances of the Risen Lord—the independence of the writers? And is it not quite conceivable that the two Evangelists give the facts as they had gathered them respectively from the only two persons who could be evidence in the matter, Joseph and Mary? St. Luke, who tells us that he had been at pains to gather information—concerning, it may be noted, "those things which were already surely believed" amongst the disciples—from those who from the beginning were eye witnesses, evidently bases his whole account of the early events and mysteries of the Incarnation on the testimony of St. Mary, who alone could have furnished him with the facts he relates—not with regard to the miraculous conception alone, but throughout his first two chapters. And with this agrees, as has been commonly noted, the different style of that portion of his narrative.* St. Matthew,

---

* St. Luke i. 5—ii. 52, being more full of Hebraisms, as would naturally be a literal rendering into Greek of an Aramaic report.

on the other hand, tells all in his first two chapters from the standpoint, as we might say, of Joseph. *

Passing from Scriptural testimony it would seem clear, both from the evidence of early Creeds and from the writings of the Fathers, that the doctrine in question was a part of the original body of Christian teaching communicated by the Apostles to the Churches they founded, before they committed their oral teaching to writing. On what other theory should we account for the agreement of all early summaries of Christian belief in declaring the Virgin Birth of the Incarnate Son ? A challenge may be safely made to produce a single document of this sort which

* The question of St. Matthew's quotation of Isaiah's prophecy (St. Matt. i. 22; Isa. vii. 14) is intentionally passed over, as raising a side issue, which, however interesting, is by no means necessary to the understanding or accepting of the Evangelist's narrative. To suppose that Matthew built his record on Isaiah's prophecy is wholly gratuitous. His phrase "that it might be fulfilled" may mean no more than that he saw in the event *a* fulfilment of the ancient prophecy, by no means to the exclusion of a more direct, historical reference. Comp. St. Matt. iv. 13 sq. and Isa. ix. 1, 2.

hints at any other mode of Birth.* Such perfect agreement in substance amid variations of expression could only arise from a common τύπος διδαχῆς † delivered to the several Churches by their Apostolic founders. Imitation in those days of comparatively scant opportunity for intercourse would have been impossible.

* It should in candour be said that the Nicene Creed in its original form did not contain any statement on the mode of our Lord's Birth, but simply affirmed that He "came down and was incarnate." The Constantinopolitan Symbol added the words, "Of the Holy Ghost and the Virgin Mary." It has been sometimes argued from this that the Virgin Birth was not regarded as of the same importance in the East as by the early Latin Church. But, not to mention other Eastern authorities, we have in Irenæus (A.D. 180), who represents both East and West, a confession of faith quite explicit on this point : "We believe . . . His Birth of a Virgin and His Passion, and His Resurrection from the dead, and the Ascension into the heavens in the flesh, of the beloved Christ Jesus our Lord," etc. And of this Creed Irenæus says, "No otherwise have the Churches in Germany believed and delivered, nor those in Spain, nor the Celts, nor those in the East, nor in Egypt, nor in Libya, nor those established in the central parts of the earth," etc. Iren. *adv. Haer.* l. i. 10. See Heurtley's *Creeds of the Western Church*, pp. 7–9, and Maclear's *Introduction to the Creeds*, pp. 15, 99, 300.

† Rom. vi. 17.

One or two quotations may be allowed from the Epistles of St. Ignatius, which in a sense combine the testimony of Fathers and of Creeds, since they give the earliest traces of the different Articles of the Creed as we know them, and as they were evidently already at that time familiar.

In his Letter to the Trallians * Ignatius bids his disciples, "Be deaf when any man speaketh to you apart from Jesus Christ, who was born of the race of David, who was the Son of Mary, who was truly born and ate and drank, was truly persecuted under Pontius Pilate, was truly crucified and died in the sight of those in Heaven and those on earth and those under the earth, Who moreover was truly raised from the dead."

So at the beginning of his Epistle to the Smyrnæans † Ignatius thanks God that those whom he is addressing are "fully persuaded as touching our Lord, that He is truly of the race of David according to the flesh, but Son of God by the Divine will and power, truly born of a Virgin and baptized by John, truly

* *Trall.* 9 (Bp. Lightfoot's translation).   † *Smyrn.* I.

nailed up in the flesh for our sakes under Pontius Pilate," etc.

It is needless to multiply citations (as might of course easily be done) to prove that from the first and throughout Christendom the Virgin Birth of our Lord was a part of Christian belief. If it was not a genuine part of Apostolic tradition, the "corrupt following of the Apostles" must indeed have begun early. And in any case the universal acceptance of the doctrine would seem, if *any* inspiration of the Christian Society by the Spirit of Truth be believed in, to determine the point. For, be it noted, this is not a question of *view* but of *fact*. It is not like views that may be taken of some generally accepted fact, which may well vary in different ages, as among minds of different degrees of intelligence; this is a question of fact, or rather (in the mind of those who do not accept the fact) of the translating of an idea (certainly not a very clear one) into an imaginary fact. Can we suppose that the whole Church, to which the guidance of the Spirit of Truth was promised, would have been allowed to make such a mistake, and on such a point, a mistake, too, that has eaten so deep into her thought and life ? The case is not parallel to any of the Old Testament stories with which some might be inclined to compare it. For (*a*) while none will contend that either St. Matthew or St. Luke were writing allegory, or supposed themselves to be aught but chroniclers of fact, (*b*) the event related was not of by-gone time but of comparatively recent occurrence when they wrote.

II. To leave the ground of testimony, let us consider the *intrinsic reasonableness* of the doctrine. Where the doctrine is doubted we may be fairly sure that the doubt springs originally not from a sense of a want of sufficient testimony, but from an uneasy feeling in the presence of the miraculous and supernatural, and a desire to minimize this element in Christian teaching.

The popular objection to miracles as *a priori* " impossible " is simply shallow. Have we come to such a clear and exhaustive understanding of the " Laws of Nature " that we can attribute to them a rigid inflexibility,—in which the idea of God is extinguished and man becomes a machine? In speaking of physical science people are in the habit of using *law* and *cause* as if they were interchangeable. But is this so? Do "the Laws of Nature" mean more than that certain phenomena are observed always to follow one another in regular sequence? Do they in any way supersede or render unnecessary for *causation* the action of a *Will?* Physical science knows nothing of the relation of cause and effect, only of antecedent and consequent. Directly we fall back on a Creative Will behind the forces of Nature, the *a priori* objection to what we call miracles has vanished. It stands to reason that such a power can¯ manipulate His own forces, can vary their direction and their results, can produce immediately results that ordinarily are mediately effected." *

What is there then against reason in the

* See Canon Malcolm MacColl's Ripon Lectures on the Nicene Creed, *Christianity in Relation to Science and Morals.* Part of his argument on this article I have done little more than condense in the preceding sentences concerning miracles.

variation, on a great occasion and for a great moral purpose, of the ordinary law of the transmission of life through two parents, especially when, as will not be disputed, we have in the present day, both in the vegetable and animal kingdoms, instances of *agamogenesis?* * For the acceptance of Miracles two things only are reasonably required,— sufficient evidence and an adequate purpose. I may quote in this connection the words of the late Archbishop Thomson in his General Introduction to the Gospels in the *Bible* [or *Speaker's*] *Commentary*, in which he shows the untenableness of many elaborate hypotheses concerning the origin of the Gospels, of one of which—"the original document" theory—he says that it "has this advantage as a theory that its facts are all derived from the mind, and are therefore practically unlimited;" the supply will always be equal to the demand.† "The argument (Dr. Thomson says) that miracles are not so much im-

* See the articles on "Bees" and on "Biology" in the *Encyclopædia Britannica.*

† Page xi.

possible as unlikely, that the testimony needs to be very strong to overcome the antecedent improbability of a miracle, has just this much truth in it, that where everything betokens that Nature is running her ordinary course, the interposition of an isolated or aimless miracle could not be looked for, or readily believed. But when Jesus was born in Bethlehem, when Jesus died on Calvary, things were not in their ordinary course. A wonderful life, and the promise of a wonderful work for man, were accompanied by wonders wrought for men." *

This point leads to the consideration of the reasonableness of the doctrine, as distinct from its possibility.

If the Catholic doctrine of the Incarnation be accepted, the miraculous conception seems to follow almost as a matter of course. The expression, " the Catholic doctrine of the Incarnation " is used, because in these days there is a good deal of writing and speaking about the Incarnation in which that word—like others—is used in a sense which, if not un-

* Page lx.

natural, is widely different from that which historically has belonged to it. If by the Incarnation is meant that on an already existing human person, Jesus, there descended in extraordinary, say in unique, measure the Divine influence, *then*, of course, the Virgin Birth is (so far as we can see) a wholly unnecessary and gratuitous addition of miracle. But if with Christendom in general, with certainly the great Creeds of Christendom, *we begin with a Divine Person*, Who, having existed from all eternity, in time was " manifested in the flesh "—then one might almost say that no other entrance into the world is imaginable than that which the Creed states to have been chosen, "Conceived by the Holy Ghost, Born of the Virgin Mary."

Thus the single Personality of the Incarnate Word is guarded; a pure and sinless Humanity is secured, exempt from transmitted evil, free from all flaw; really one with us in nature, being formed from the substance of the Virgin Mother, while that which was taken *from* her was wholly fashioned *by* the Spirit of God. St. Paul's doctrine of "the Second Adam" (Who is "from Heaven"), a fresh starting-point of renewed humanity, would seem really to require the supernatural conception of Him Who is so designated.*

The same may fairly be urged with respect to the absolute Sinlessness of Christ— "Holy, harmless, undefiled, and separate from sinners," the "Lamb without blemish and without spot"—which is constantly insisted on by the Apostolic writers.† Thus intimately and delicately are truths related one to another. Of this a word more presently.

* 1 Cor. xv. 45; comp. the argument in Rom. v. 12 sq. and 2 Cor. v. 14, 15 (R. V.).

† Heb. vii. 26; 1 Pet. i. 19.

Concerning the *Single and Divine Personality* of our Lord, see Liddon's Bampton Lectures, pp. 262–7, and the Christmas-day Sermon in the second volume of Newman's Sermons. The following passage, at once eloquent and exact, may be quoted from the Introduction to Dr. Bright's Addresses on *The Seven Sayings from the Cross*, pp. 10, 11:

Who, then, is He, the Jesus of the Passion? He is not a preëminent saint, who responded with a signal readiness to the Divine voice, who realized more worthily than other men "the Divine idea" of human excellence, and to whom, by a laxity of phrase not free from profaneness, men might

Here let me quote a paragraph from a sermon of Dr. Liddon's on the subject (in his Christmastide volume) * in which he deals with a point often urged in this connection, and (as was his wont) acutely claims as an argument for the truth that which was adduced as an objection.

Doubtless, here and there in the heathen world, there were legends of sages or poets who were born of virgins; but these legends are related to the history of our Saviour's Birth, as are false to true miracles. As the counterfeit miracle implies the real miracle of which it is a counterfeit, so the idea of virgin birth, here and there discoverable in Paganism, points to a deep instinct of the human race,

---

thus ascribe a so-called " moral divinity." No, He is literally and essentially Divine; He is "the only-begotten Son of God," that is, the one Son by nature, and, because He is thus Son, is "God from God." The "I" in Him, His very Self, His Personality, is Divine, not human; yet has He condescended, in His miraculous love, to take our humanity into union with His Person, to assume as His own, from the first moment of their existence, a human body and soul; and this without the slightest germ of sin, without any possibility of deviation, in the movements of that soul, from the will of the Eternal Father, but with all the innocent instincts and affections of our nature, so that, while remaining unchangeably God, He could also be "a High Priest able to sympathize with our infirmities," etc.

* Serm. vi. " Born of a Virgin," pp. 95, 96.

and to a high probability that the absolute religion would
satisfy it. Men felt, Pagans though they were, the oppres-
sion and degradation of their hereditary nature; they longed
for some break in the tyrannical traditions of flesh and blood;
they longed for the appearance of some being who should
still belong to them, yet in a manner so exceptional as to be
able to inaugurate a new era in humanity. Revelation,
surely, is not less trustworthy because it recognizes an instinct which only led men to do it justice, and which was in
accordance with moral truth.

In regard to another line of thought
which has been (curiously, as I must think)
urged as antagonistic to the doctrine of the
Incarnation, as the Church hath received the
same, including this subsidiary point which
we are considering—the theory or doctrine
of Evolution, I should like to refer to Bishop
H. M. Thompson's clever and eloquent use
of this very theory to illustrate the unique
character and person of Christ, in the fourth
of his "Bishop Paddock Lectures" on *The
World and The Kingdom*. "The Child in
the Manger" is the title of the lecture.
"There is a half truth (he says) in the
thought of those who imagine the Faith a
development. There is a half truth in every
falsehood. The Divine Religion has its

human side as well as its divine. The
'treasure,' in the largest sense, is in earthen
vessels. The *environment* for Christ and
for Christianity is developed in what we
blindly call the natural order, but *the environment does not make Christ.*" The analogy
is perfect between His character and teaching, and His Person.

III. I have already more than once hinted
at a part of the answer which I should make
to the last question, which it was proposed
to consider,—*Cui bono?* What is the moral
value of a belief in the Virgin-Birth of
Christ? Supposing it to be true, what does
a man lose who fails to accept it? What relation has it to conduct? How can it be
counted among beliefs necessary to salvation?

1. The reply which has been already par-
tially anticipated is this. Truths have an
indirect as well as a direct value. Supposing some to be themselves without immedi-
ate bearing on life and conduct, they may
guard and protect other truths which have a

direct and tremendous moral import. For instance, in this case, the Virgin-Birth I should regard as an integral part of the true doctrine of the Incarnation, as witnessing to our Lord's unique Personality, His sinless and representative manhood, His perfect sacrifice.

2. Then, again, the analogy between our Lord's Incarnate life and the spiritual life of His people ought not to be overlooked. The teaching of the New Testament writers, of St. Paul more especially, taken up into the devotional thought of the Church, and embodied in much of our Prayer-Book language, is that each mystery of the Lord's Incarnate life has its counterpart in the spiritual experience of the faithful. For us He was born, that we might be reborn in Him. For us He died, that with Him we might die to sin and self. For us He rose again, that in Him we might rise to newness of life. And *how* was He born? "Conceived by the Holy Ghost, Born of the Virgin Mary." It is the law of spiritual birth, for the formation of Divine life within the

soul. "Not by might nor by power"—not by human resources, or natural means, "but by My Spirit, saith the Lord of hosts." From first to last our sanctification is the work of the Holy Spirit, by His preventing and assisting grace. No friend or minister can do more than Gabriel did, or Joseph— *announce* God's message, to which the soul must itself respond with self-surrender, that the Spirit may accomplish His work, and then *guard* the life of grace which has been by His overshadowing communicated.

www.ingramcontent.com/pod-product-compliance
Lightning Source LLC
Chambersburg PA
CBHW020115030726
47498CB00006B/2116